MW01093254

Son, We Need to Talk

SON, WE NEED TO TALK

Coping with My Son's Suicide

LeRoy Lawson

FOREWORD BY
Mark A. Taylor

CASCADE *Books* • Eugene, Oregon

SON, WE NEED TO TALK
Coping with My Son's Suicide

Cascade Books
An Imprint of Wipf and Stock Publishers
199 W. 8th Ave., Suite 3
Eugene, OR 97401

www.wipfandstock.com

PAPERBACK ISBN: 978-1-6667-6138-2
HARDCOVER ISBN: 978-1-6667-6139-9
EBOOK ISBN: 978-1-6667-6140-5

Cataloguing-in-Publication data:

Names: Lawson, LeRoy [author]. | Taylor, Mark A. [foreword writer].

Title: Son, we need to talk : coping with my son's suicide / by LeRoy
Lawson ; foreword by Mark A. Taylor.

Description: Eugene, OR: Cascade Books, 2023.

Identifiers: ISBN 978-1-6667-6138-2 (paperback) | ISBN 978-1-6667-
6139-9 (hardcover) | ISBN 978-1-6667-6140-5 (ebook)

Subjects: LCSH: Suicide—Religious aspects—Christianity. | Depressed
persons—Religious life. | Grief—Religious aspects—Christianity. |
Pastoral care.

Classification: BV4012.2 L39 2023 (print) | BV4012.2 (ebook)

06/01/23

From the first days until now, my unfailing source
of support and encouragement has been my family.

In the beginning there was Joy. God joined us in 1960,
"for better or for worse, for richer or for poorer, in sick-
ness and in health." We've experienced it all—together.

Then there were our children, Kimberly, Candace,
and Lane, gifts without compare.

Then there were the sons-in-law, the grandchildren,
and their loved ones

Then the great-grandchildren

And from nearly the beginning, all the large Velcro
family, dozens strong, held together not by blood
but by a love that will not let go.

I am grateful to have been pastor and professor,
a writer and speaker and leader of sorts.

I am most grateful of all to have been *pater familias*
to this incredible group.

Son, We Need to Talk is for them.

Contents

Foreword

Listening in on a Conversation
We Need to Hear

NOT MANY KNOW THE grief of losing a child: the disbelief, the anger, the sense of being cheated out of seeing this special person continue to grow and flourish. Any death is hard, but seldom do we invest the nurture, hope, and pride we give to our own flesh and blood. When all that we cherished about this person is stolen and destroyed, little can take the place of what we've lost.

And when the death is by suicide, our loss is complicated by nagging self-doubt and questions, so many unanswered questions.

When Roy and Joy Lawson lost their twenty-six-year-old son Lane they faced all these emotions and more. If only they'd had the chance for one more long talk, one more opportunity to listen and to reassure. It was as if someone had pulled the plug on a vital conversation.

They've kept their thoughts and longing for Lane in their hearts for the almost three decades since the policeman knocked at their door in the middle of the night to say Lane's body had been found. And Roy has tried to get it all out in words typed into his computer. Soon his writing took the form of a conversation with Lane. With only the short note Lane left behind, Roy wrote responses to every phrase, every claim, every explanation Lane offered.

But it wasn't easy. Putting all this into some form that would make sense to himself, let alone to another reader, was too painful. Time and again, Roy closed the file and pushed his conversation aside, but he couldn't forget it. This was a talk that needed to be finished.

Finally, he has succeeded in coming to terms with the darkness that drove Lane to suicide. Finally, he is satisfied with his effort to express how he always loved Lane and why the pain of losing him will never completely go away.

Here, in this book, is that dialogue. Lane can't read it, of course, but you and I can. And in so doing, we will discover meaning and perspective to enrich our understanding of life even as we grieve with Roy over this death.

Those who have lost a child as Roy has will resonate with his emotions.

Those who do not know what it means to confront such a loss will gain new understanding to comfort others whose child decided to leave them.

Every reader will come away with hope, understanding that one death need not kill our own resolve to embrace the complications and the beauty of life.

—Mark A. Taylor

Preface

"DAD, WE NEED TO talk."

I can hear them yet. When the three Lawson children were still in the nest, their preacher-professor father kept an office at home. It was my hideaway for preparing sermons, outlining lectures, composing often-long-overdue answers to usually-but-not-always-patient correspondents, and attacking the stack of must-read books. None of these chores is what I now remember most, though. Instead, I picture Kim or Candy or Lane appearing at the door to announce in all seriousness, "Dad, we need to talk." I often thought, but never said, "The truth is, *we* don't need to talk, but it sounds like *you* do." That was good enough. I'd find a place to pause what I was doing—my wife, Joy, says she can't remember the children having to wait more than ten minutes—and we'd talk. I'm so glad we did.

Lane, the youngest, died by his own hand on May 26, 1994, one month short of his twenty-seventh birthday. Has there been even a day since that I haven't said, "Son, we need to talk"? Oh, I know, *we* don't need to, but *I* do. It comes with fatherhood, I suppose, and certainly gets ramped up in my profession, this compulsion to probe, to explain—to have the last word. The truth is, I really do *need* to talk.

Lane's letter was a good one, if there can be such a thing as a good suicide note, but in spite of his best intentions his last words raised as many questions as they answered. One especially haunted his father, the one about love. If ever a person loved and was loved, he was that person. If ever love alone could defeat suicide, it should have come to Lane's rescue.

But one of the toughest lessons his suicide taught us is this: Love isn't enough. Not by itself. Life requires faith, too. And hope.

Time has brought some solace, but the yearning to talk hasn't gone away. So we've been talking, Lane and I, for decades now. He still has the last word, but this book tells you *now* what I would have said to him *then*, if I could have. My son speaks from his final letter, the father answers from his grieving heart.

I began writing this little book many years ago. Every time I reread it, I fiddle with the wording, trying to be clearer, more succinct. The writing has evolved with time; the emotions haven't. I'm almost surprised each time I return to these pages by how little they have changed since then. The same sense of loss, of puzzlement, and of longing for another chance to talk with my son grips me. I can't stop the tears. I reread carefully, mentally arguing with him, challenging his reasoning, doing my best even now to change his mind, to prevent his terrible act, to rewrite history. But of course I can't. What's done is done.

But we still need to talk.

At least I do.

Lane Whitney Lawson, High School Graduation

Goodbye,

I've been writing this, my final missive, for about a week now. I've got a lot to say, since this is my last chance, and I want to answer as many of the possible questions as I can so as to elevate you of the inevitable questioning period that follows this sort of thing.

First off, let me say I'm sorry. Sorry for the mess I've left (not the least of which is the present condition of my room.) Sorry for the pain this will cause. And just plain sorry for being such a mess.

The causes are many. I hate the pain. I hate the fuzzy brain. I hate that because of these I can't really hope to accomplish much. The things I live for are taken away. I can't fully attend to any of because of both problems. My piano practice is a torture of attempting to focus and feeling my fore-arms swell because of use. I essentially live for others because whatever I do wears me out. I enjoy making people laugh, but that tires my brain. In everything I do there is a restriction caused by my body. I can't eat what I want. I can't breathe most air. I can't cope with the day to day. All this coupled with a minimal at best will to live just doesn't make sense any more.

I'm totally unemotional about my own demise. The only time I get choked up is envisioning you all getting the news.

I truly do regret that, but I've lived for you long enough. I guess I'm being selfish, but at least I won't have to live with the guilt trip (sorry for the morbid jokes, but I can't deny myself a few final smiles).

I don't want any stupid blaming of yourself. As you well know I do my own thing with minimal adherence to counsel. Besides, if none of you is a closet psychic healer, there's not a thing to be done. I can't just take up space on this planet, I require a contribution of myself. Since none is forthcoming...

I'm also curious about what's next. It's got to be better than this, but I won't know till I'm there. I hope there's no afterlife or reincarnation, because I'm ready to just be dead.

Geez, just writing this is making my shoulder burn.

Don't be sad for me. This is what I most need. Don't grieve to long for yourselves, get on with your life. Raise an occasional glass of wine or beer (my personal recommendation is the Morton Cadet Cabernet Sauvignon) to my memory, and strive to be happy since I couldn't.

More practical thoughts keep coming to mind, so I'd better get them out of the way. ▪ Regarding my funeral, I want the least amount spent as possible. Plain wood box. Smallest possible headstone (6"x6" is what comes to mind) inscribed "Boys to the end."

Well, I went back down and sent some money to Dianne. And a message to come look for my body. Terrible way to do it, but I wanted to make sure she got the money, and that I was found before I rotted too much. I also had a pretty good last meal, all the things I'm not supposed to eat. Didn't come up with a reason not to go through with this, so here I am again.

Some more questions.

Why before Hawaii? I figured I'd just spend the money someone else could use. I'd be consumed by the thoughts of doing this all the while, so I wouldn't really enjoy myself. Besides, I woke up this morning so bad off I really don't care. No time like the present, eh?

Why not wait for antidepressants? I don't like em, and they wouldn't stop the pain. I don't figure the yeast stuff is really going to help either. Better to just let someone who wants to live fill the gap I leave.

If I love you, why? Would you really rather I lived like this? Better to put your worries at rest also.

Why here? I like this campground. Plus I figured I won't be stopped here, and I'll be found soon enough. It's nice and shady so my body won't get to hot and get nasty.

Why this way?
I was going to use the gun, but that's
pretty gross to find. Believe it or not
I'm trying to be as thoughtful as this
sort of thing allows.

Enough writing. Again, I'm really sorry.
Please forgive me. Have a great life
I'm on to better things, so don't worry
about me. No more pain, yeah!

I Love You,

Jane

.

I

THE LETTER

[*May 26, 1994*
but undated]

Goodbye,

I've been writing this, my final missive, for about a week now. I've got a lot to say, since this is my last chance, and I want to answer as many of the possible questions as I can so as to alleviate you of the inevitable questioning period that follows this sort of thing.

First off, let me say I'm sorry. Sorry for the mess I've left (not the least of which is the present condition of my room). Sorry for the pain this will cause. And just plain sorry for being such a wuss.

The causes are many. I hate the pain. I hate the fuzzy brain. I hate that because of these I can't really hope to accomplish much. The things I live for are taken away. I can't fully attend Gung-fu because of both problems. My piano practice is a torture of attempting to focus and feeling my forearms swell because of use. I essentially live for others because whatever I do wears me out. I enjoy making people laugh, but that tires my brain. In everything I do there is a restriction caused by my body. I can't eat what I want. I can't breathe most air. I can't cope with the day to day. All this coupled with a minimal at best will to live just doesn't make sense anymore.

I'm totally unemotional about my own demise. The only time I get choked up is envisioning you all getting the news. I truly regret that, but I've lived for you long enough. I guess I'm being selfish, but at least I won't have to live with the guilt trip (sorry for the morbid jokes but I can't deny myself a few final smirks.)

I don't want any stupid blaming of yourself. As you well know I do my own thing with minimal adherence to counsel. Besides, if none of you is a closet psychic healer, there's not a thing to be done. I can't just take up space on this planet. I require a contribution of myself. Since none is forthcoming . . .

I'm also curious about what's next. It's got to be better than this, but I won't know till I'm there. I hope there's no afterlife or reincarnation, because I'm ready to just be dead.

Geez, just writing this is making my shoulder burn.

Don't be sad for me. This is what I most need. Don't grieve too long for yourselves, get on with your life. Raise an occasional glass of wine or beer (my personal recommendation is the Mouton Cadet Cabernet Sauvignon) to my memory, and strive to be happy since I couldn't.

More practical thoughts keep coming to mind, so I'd better get them out of the way. Regarding my funeral, I want the least amount spent as possible. Plain wood box. Smallest possible (6" by 6" is what comes to mind) inscribed "Bozo to the end." No funeral parlor. No rehashing of my little life, boiling it down to its meaningless essence. Just say a few words and drop me in the cheapest plot available. If it is cheaper . . . have me cremated and toss my ashes. Who wants a morbid urn hanging around? I want my death like my life; short, to the point, minimalist, and humorous if you can manage.

Sell off my stuff to pay for it. I would like my radio and music to go to Dianne. I'd also like her to get at least a grant ($1,000) if my "estate" can do that. You may not know it, but she is the love of my life. I'm sorry for the unsurmountable obstacles between us, and that we got together when I'd had it. She's an incredibly wonderful person, one of the best I've ever known. She gets whatever she wants of my stuff. The antiques at the store are mine, so keep what you want and sell the rest. Try to cash the AT&T check that will come shortly to give to Dianne. The piano goes to Albert

Williams my piano teacher. Leave my finances in the ruin I left them, and use my stuff for a little fun yourselves.

I love my family, greatest people on Earth, sorry I couldn't hang with you longer.

Well, I went back and sent some money to Dianne. And a message to come look for my body. Terrible way to do it, but I wanted to make sure she got the moola and that I was found before I rotted too much. I also had a pretty good last meal, all the things I'm not supposed to eat. Didn't come up with a reason not to go through with this, so here I am again.

Some more questions.

Why before Hawaii? I figured I'd just spend the money someone else could use. I'd be consumed by the thoughts of doing this all the while, so I wouldn't really enjoy myself. Besides, I woke up this morning so bad off I really don't care. No time like the present, eh?

Why not wait for antidepressants? I don't like 'em, and they wouldn't stop the pain. I don't figure the yeast stuff is really going to help either. Better to just let someone who wants to live fill the gap I leave.

If I love you, why? Would you really rather I lived like this? Better to put your worries to rest also.

Why here?

I like this campground. Plus I figured I wouldn't be stopped here, and I'll be found soon enough. It's nice and shady so my body won't get too hot and get nasty.

Why this way?

I was going to use the gun, but that's pretty gross to find. Believe it or not I'm trying to be as thoughtful as this sort of thing allows.

Enough writing. Again, I'm really sorry. Please forgive me. Have a great life. I'm on to better things, so don't worry about me. No more pain, yeah!

I love you.

Lane

II

THE CONVERSATION

O, but they say the tongues of dying men
Enforce attention like deep harmony.
Where words are scarce, they are seldom spent in vain;
For they breathe truth that breathe their words—in pain.
—Shakespeare, *King Richard II*, II, 1.

LANE GETS THE FIRST word in this conversation. He thought it would be his final word. He couldn't have anticipated his father would still be trying to make sense of it all, searching for the words I should have said if I could have said them. Like Shakespeare's John of Gaunt, Lane's words continue to "enforce attention." I keep pondering them, probing for insight, arguing and explaining and wishing it could be otherwise. One thing is certain: his words were not "spent in vain; for they breathe truth."

The conversation begins:

> *Goodbye,*
>
> *I've been writing this, my final missive, for about a week now. I've got a lot to say, since this is my last chance, and I want to answer as many of the possible questions as I can so as to alleviate you of the inevitable questioning period that follows this sort of thing.*

"*My final missive.*" On first rereading your letter, Son, when I took time to weigh every word, I rather irrelevantly thought of

John of Gaunt in Shakespeare's *Richard II*. You used to have fun at the expense of dying heroes and heroines in dramas—especially in operas—reenacting their amazing ability to keep on talking or singing several more pages of the score before finally collapsing. John died like that, garrulous to the end, compelled to lay some more sage advice on his young king. Richard, of course, didn't pay much attention to the old man, which, I'm discovering as a very old man myself, is pretty much par for the course.

John of Gaunt's death has nothing to do with yours, I admit, except that, like his, your parting words were also delivered in pain. Unlike King Richard, though, your old father has been paying very close attention to your final words. And profiting from them.

I've read several suicide notes. Yours is the kindest I've seen, and the most helpful. Your words have haunted me for years; only now, nearly three decades later, am I finally ready to answer. You wrote down your thoughts in two sittings. My response has required much, much longer. I began these pages twelve months after you left us. I'm still returning to them, listening, searching, weighing, wishing. Your words "breathed truth." They did, indeed, "enforce attention."

I appreciate your trying to answer "as many of the possible questions" as you could, but you failed to ease the "inevitable questioning period" that follows "this sort of thing." You couldn't. Your explanations sound more like rationalizations; they raise more issues than they resolve. Mom and I have tried not to torture ourselves with the inevitable "Why?" or "How could he?" or "How is it possible?" But we haven't been able to shake them off, either. I confess that my mind was more at ease in the immediate aftershock than it was a year later, when I started writing this letter in answer to yours. Then I was numb; there were only a few nagging questions. But after the anesthetic of shock wore off, the bedeviling probing began and just wouldn't stop. Still hasn't stopped. Every glance at one of your pictures forced me to wonder again, "Does this look like a person who could take his own life?" Your unselfconscious good looks, your athletic frame, your warm eyes, your apparent zest for life are all there, a constant reminder of how your presence filled a room. Your personality energized every conversation. I am as baffled as ever.

"*My final missive . . .*" Other people write letters. You pen missives. Even in this greeting your love of language comes through. You used to worry so much about your mind. You struggled to force it to work for you when your allergies clouded your thinking, complicating the simple processing of information into major, exhausting projects. In elementary school you would sometimes complain your brain seemed divided. You couldn't make both sides function together, you said. But here's evidence that even when your depression was at its worst, you could still fight your way to the proper word, the slight touch of wit to lighten the tone of this, the heaviest of essays.

The precise word you could usually find; with your spelling ("aleviate," for example) you were not always as successful. It remained uniquely yours.

Lane on The Rock, contemplating

"*. . . for about a week now.*" Sometimes a person hates to be right. Already in this first sentence you confirm that our fears were not misplaced. Our suspicions were justified. Yours was not death by impulse. You were firming up your plans even as you were deny-ing them to your mother and sister. "Don't worry," you said. "I'm not going to do anything foolish," you said to your mother regularly and to Candy in your last phone conversation with her. Just ambiguous enough to disarm. If we could ask you now, you'd still insist, "But it *wasn't* foolish of me to take my life. It was the wisest course of action under the circumstances, the only attractive one open to me. It might seem foolish to you, but that's because you aren't able to see through my eyes. You don't feel my body's pain."

You also knew that suicide was inconceivable to us. No, that's not quite accurate. Inconceivable to me, not to your mother. She struggled through too many years with her own version of your illness not to understand. When I asked her, after you were gone, whether she had ever considered suicide, she said, "No, but I've often thought that if I didn't wake up in the morning, it would be okay." Her religious convictions ruled out death by her own hand, but her aching body and sometimes foggy mind would have wel-comed the relief of no more tomorrows.

Your "I won't do anything foolish" didn't give her the as-surance it gave me. She heard the depression in your voice when you called home. She identified with your struggle, and it scared her. She already had a trip to Oregon planned, but she promptly changed her scheduled flight so she could get to you sooner. She phoned our family doctor and friend Karen Nichols to ask that medicine be sent at once. Dr. Nichols dispatched it that day. (We found the pills in your mailbox at the post office when we got to Oregon.) Having tended to your medical needs and a few other chores, Mom would be ready to leave right after Memorial Day. She then called to tell you when to expect her.

You knew she was coming. You knew the medicine was in the mail.

You couldn't wait.

In spite of what you knew—or because of it—you drove to the forest campground and hooked up that cursed hose. Sorry, but if this wasn't foolish—at least from your family's point of view—what should we call it?

The forest he loved—and chose to die in

First off, let me say I'm sorry for the mess I've left (not the least of which is the present condition of my room). Sorry for the pain this will cause. And just plain sorry for being such a wuss.

Your room *was* a mess. We didn't see it at its worst. Your roommate Jeff had already cleaned it up by the time we got there. He's a more fastidious type than you. But then, almost everybody is. Jeff went into some detail about how he had picked up, sorted, made things ready for us to take away when we arrived. He didn't need to explain.

Neat you have never been. Sensitive to the feelings of others, though, and conscientious in easing their pain, you have always been, so when you say you're sorry, we believe you. And now we're sorry.

About the other messes you mention. Yes, your personal finances were a bit bewildering. I didn't realize then, in the first few weeks after you left us, that I'd still be dealing with some of your creditors a year later. I paid every one I knew about. I hope I got them all.

SON, WE NEED TO TALK

Then there was the matter of your thrift store partner. You didn't choose the best person to go into business with, I'm afraid. She told us she had gone to your place to clean your room before we got there, but her real purpose was to look for the key to your storage unit. She found it—and stripped it bare. Then to us she denied there ever was a storage room. We knew the truth, because you had earlier told your mother about it. Our brief dealings with her gave us insight into what you must have had to put up with. We experienced her as a selfish, calloused, dishonest person. You had let us know your business venture with her was discouraging. Now we knew why.

The money you left went, as you directed, to Dianne. She wouldn't keep it. In spite of her own straitened finances, she donated it to the Lane Whitney Lawson Memorial Scholarship Fund we established at Pacific Christian College (now Hope International University). "I think from his new perspective, this is what Lane would want me to do with the money," she explained.

Unlike your choice of business partner, you showed keen judgment in teaming up with Dianne. She's your last gift to us. We correspond. We have visited her when we're in Oregon. She came to be with us for a few days in Arizona. Getting to know her compounded our confusion. When we first met, I told her, "I know why Lane fell in love with you. You're his mother." I didn't mean you were seeking a mother figure, which she may have thought at first. No, it's that she's so much like your mother I found myself staring. Same soft eyes, fair complexion, quiet voice, natural poise and dignity. Then, as we got to know her better, the resemblance seemed even stronger: same steady faith, same understated wisdom, same capacity for love. To leave her—well, you had to have been desperate.

Thanks to Dianne's generosity, everything, even the money you knew she needed, went into your scholarship fund. The bills that kept popping up? Your mother and I paid them. They weren't large and they weren't numerous. A magazine subscription here, a still pending medical bill there, the return of the portion of your monthly disability check the company demanded since you didn't "work" all the days they paid for. (You couldn't have; you were already gone.) Small things, little messes.

". . . *for being such a wuss.*" Here we do have to argue with you. You are being unfair. You weren't a wuss. To the contrary, you were, to our admittedly biased minds, extraordinary. You were one of those rare individuals who light up every room you walk into. We have seen that all your life, of course. What we didn't know until too late was how much you had charmed your adopted town of Brookings. They talked to us, your friends there, of your wit, your laughter, your friendliness, your charisma. Like us, they didn't guess the extent of your pain. Your sudden death shocked them, too. They didn't see a "wuss" but a young man who "really had it together," they said, one who was overcoming his physical disability through self-discipline and personal courage.

Practicing tai chi at his grandparents' home

I read somewhere that male suicide can be attributed to a man's perception that he has lost status among other men, that he no longer regards himself a real man among men. That this was not your situation was proved immediately after you left us.

Your friends turned out in large numbers for your memorial service. A few of them addressed the rest of us mourners, describing the skills you exhibited in the children's *tai chi* classes you taught. They spoke of your articles the local paper published. They praised your spontaneous unselfishness. We didn't hear a word about your being "a wuss," and certainly as nothing less than a *real* man.

I wish we could have voted on your decision. The vote would have been Everybody to One. You didn't give us a chance even to debate the motion.

"Sorry for the pain I've caused." Yes, you are right on this one. You've left *us* a mess. We've run the emotional gamut: shock, denial, anguish, anger, guilt, resignation, uncertainty, and—surprisingly—eventually a kind of peace, the kind that comes with the reluctant admission, "It is what it is." The passing of time hasn't helped as much as might be expected, though. Almost the opposite. We don't cry as often as during the first few months. After a while the tears came less copiously but sometimes just as uncontrollably. They have never disappeared entirely. Every time I have sat at my desk to prepare this manuscript for publication, my blurred vision forces me to stop, wipe my eyes, take a deep breath and begin again.

Almost anything will trigger them—catching a glimpse of a blond-headed young man crossing the street half a block away, a childhood picture of you sent by a friend, a touching scene in a movie. I've tried including a reminiscence of you in a sermon from time to time, but then I sometimes unexpectedly choke up before I'm halfway through the story. How many times, in preparing a sermon, I thought I might include a personal anecdote as the ideal illustration of the point I wanted to make. Then, because it was about *you*, I had to delete it. I couldn't be trusted not to break. After all these years, I'm still uncertain of myself.

The crying may be less frequent, but the ache in our hearts burrowed deep and took permanent residence there, lurking until, in an unguarded moment, the tears rush to the surface, unbidden, without warning. People don't like to see a grown man cry. (At least, this grown man hates it when *this* grown man cries!) So I talk about you less than I want to.

The worst pain is in not being able to see you again, to look forward to your coming home for the holidays, to talk this whole thing over—to hug you. It's physical, this yearning. We've always been demonstrative. I thought that was good. I still do, but oh, the ache they leave behind when the hugs depart for good. Only a couple of months after you left, your mother put it into words for both of us. "What is getting me is the never-againness," she said. She believes in heaven, but at that moment heaven was far from her mind. She wanted you here, now, to touch, to hold, to look at and laugh with. Just to be with. Me too.

We know you are sorry for the pain you've caused. We're sorry for the pain that led you to cause it. We feel more sorrow for your pain than ours, but ours is very real, too. We also are convinced that if you had guessed just how much anguish your decision inflicted you wouldn't have done it, even if it meant continuing to live with your own hurt. We believe that, because all your life you hated other people's wounds as much as your own. Yes, we ache, but one hurt we don't have: the pain some parents bear when their children choose to hurt others. "Be kind to one another" is a scripture you took seriously.

> *The causes are many. I hate the pain. I hate the fuzzy brain. I hate that because of these I can't really hope to accomplish much. The things I live for are taken away. I can't fully attend Gung-fu because of both problems. My piano practice is a torture of attempting to focus and feeling my fore arms swell because of use. I essentially live for others because whatever I do wears me out. I enjoy making people laugh, but that tires my brain. In everything I do there is a restriction caused by my body. I can't eat what I want. I can't breathe most air. I can't cope with the*

day to day. All this coupled with a minimal at best will to
live just doesn't make sense any more.

You were eight when we first recognized the symptoms of the Lawson Family Illness. Your older sister Kim fortunately escaped, but Candy showed her first signs when she was four. Your mother also struggled for at least a couple of decades with a vague, un-defined malady that would only be diagnosed when one of you children's pediatricians looked up from you and told her she had the same issue. "I can see it in your eyes," he said. "Neuro-chemical depression," her psychiatrist eventually named it.

She had been searching for years for somebody who could tell her what was wrong. This was the label he gave her. Other doctors variously tagged it Epstein-Barr Syndrome, chronic fa-tigue syndrome, candida, yeast, allergies to certain foods, hyper-activity, and so on. The years helped us to isolate the cause more accurately. As with your mother and sister, your greatest enemies were petrochemicals—and they were everywhere: in the clothes you wore, the furniture you sat on, the chemicals you worked with. Worst of all, the pervasive byproduct of the automotive age, they were in the air you breathed.

So as a young man you moved from Arizona to Oregon, first to your grandparents' cabin in Port Orford and then after a while to Brookings, to be closer to your *tai chi* classes. Even in Oregon, though, cars and trucks spewed their poisons, diminishing the ef-fect of the pure ocean breezes. And even there, clothes (with their synthetic fabrics) and chemicals ganged up against you as well.

We were unaware, until your friends there told us, how se-verely your body was deteriorating in those last days. Dianne said you were having difficulty swallowing. A *tai chi* buddy said you entered your last competition with your right arm and shoulder virtually useless. Not until we read your letter did we discover that playing the piano hurt so much, nor did we realize that your eating had once again become a trial. So much we didn't know.

I hate the fuzzy brain. This sentence takes me back to your grade school years. We began observing mood swings then, although we didn't call them that. You would become morose, defeatist, tearful. When we'd ask about how you were feeling, you'd explain you seemed to be disengaged from your own mental processes, as if you were standing apart, an outside observer of your own behavior. You couldn't think clearly, you complained. Paranoia took over. "Nobody likes me. I'm no good," you told us—as an eight-year-old!

These became familiar refrains in grade school. I thought for a while you were going through a phase and would outgrow it. (That's how my parents wrote off my childhood complaints: "You're just going through a phase. You'll get over it.") You weren't outgrowing it, though, and you didn't get over it.

In high school the story was the same. You confused me. How could such a handsome young man, easily attracting friends by your normally sunny disposition, whose intelligence shone through everything you tried, feel worthless and unloved? Your hyperactive father didn't understand. I sometimes thought you must be lazy. "Straighten up," I'd explain. I wanted you to see "things just aren't that bad." But to you they were.

Lane having fun with high school friends Brad, Mike, and Dirk

In our father-son discussions, I became the student. You taught me to doubt my powers of discernment. I had to admit I wasn't good at reading another person's thoughts and moods. When you spoke of your fuzzy brain, your mother understood and tried to help me to. I said I could comprehend what you two were talking about, but I guess I couldn't. I've often had difficulty concentrating, especially when my own allergies are raging. But you weren't talking about lack of concentration. You were describing fuzziness, unfocused-ness, lethargy bordering on mental paralysis, an inability to process incoming information, and a loss of motivation to try.

When in that state, both as a child and later as an adult, you felt you couldn't accomplish anything, couldn't organize your thoughts, couldn't plan. You could barely cope with the immediate. The mind simply wouldn't cooperate and even when it would, the body would often rebel. That's why you sometimes idled as hours and days and even weeks wasted away, you who so desperately wanted to do something with your life, to release the potential you knew you had but couldn't realize.

After years of effort, your "minimal at best will to live" wasn't enough. You quit trying.

"If it's worth starting, it's worth finishing," your grandfather reminded me again and again when I was a boy. He got through to me. Ever since childhood I've felt compelled to finish the task, even when I began to doubt whether the task was worth starting in the first place. To this day I read even the most mediocre book to the last page. Magazines have to be devoured cover to cover. Jobs aren't to be left until they're completed.

Oh, I've quit some, to be sure, but I still mentally beat myself up for walking away from them—like that summer in college when I abruptly quit working for a landscape gardener because I couldn't stand being yelled at. He was a dry alcoholic, an irascible boss. After all these years I remain convinced I was right to leave; he was impossible to please. That was in 1957, but I'm still feeling the need to justify myself.

"If it's worth starting, it's worth finishing," Dad insisted.

I should have caught on to your condition sooner. There was a pattern, begun in childhood, of tasks unfinished. You were a quick study in anything you attempted, at first. But then your mood would shift and your initial enthusiasm turned to—what? Was it boredom? Discouragement? Disgust? Laziness? (I remember wondering whether your problem wasn't one common to other highly intelligent people: if you couldn't get it right the first time, you couldn't be bothered with it.) Whatever it was, you were through. In school you played the piano, for a while. And the trombone, for a while. Then the French horn. And the drums. Then no more music. Little league baseball held you, and so did wrestling and football, all for a while. College was appealing, for a year or two. Then on to your position with AT&T, until you had to go on disability because of your illness. About AT&T: While waiting to be interviewed for your job at AT&T, you sold a phone and a computer. You got the job. We've loved telling that story. It seems so *you*.

Stars on Lane's Little League cap are for winning every game.

Port Orford and Brookings offered new hope, for a while. Your pursuit of martial arts was fun for you, and your achievements multiplied. Then you established the thrift store, a means of gaining some independence and steeling yourself against the day when your disability checks would dry up. But everything was turning sour on you at once. The sense of accomplishment deserted again. And you quit trying.

Firsts found in fight

Lane Lawson is heading to Eugene for a martial arts tournament in June, but last month he surprised his Brookings club by coming home with some medals.

Lawson brought back eight different trophies from two martial arts tournaments in April.

On the way to visiting his grandparents in Salem, Lawson stopped in for the Chinese Martial Arts Association Tournament at Stayton, April 17.

There he won four events and took a third in another.

The Gung Fu student from Brookings-Harbor won in forms, in Tai Chi, in weapons

The Pilot/Jerry Teague

Lane Lawson, from Brookings-Harbor, won four martial arts events in Stayton and another in Eugene plus thirds.

forms with a staff and in sparring. His third-place finish came in open forms.

Then a week later Lawson competed at Choi's Oregon State Tae Kwon Do Champions and won first in color-belt forms, a third in weapons and in middle-weight sparring.

"Not bad for one-and-a-half years training at the club," said Sifu Jon Loren, the Brookings club's chief instructor. "Especially when the Gung-fu club trains for street self-defense and not tournament competition."

Brookings, Oregon, newspaper on Lane's tai chi achievements

As I'm writing these words, I'm afraid I'm sounding critical. I'm not, not at all. I'm just still searching, trying to understand what physical or psychological forces drove you to resign from life, what awful discouragement could erase the pride we who didn't live in your skin felt in your achievements. You had good friends, endless possibilities in the vocation and avocations you were giving yourself to, a beautiful woman who loved you, and a doting family that couldn't get enough of you. You lived in one of the world's beauty spots. And you abandoned them all.

I can't cope with the day to day.

Here is at least your partial answer to my puzzlement. I'm trying to understand how you could give up the future. You could, you want us to understand, because you couldn't see any way to get through the present. *"I can't cope."* There's the rub. Dad's preachments, Mom's nostrums, your friends' cheering were of no avail. You couldn't take them in. Did you ever think, "That's easy enough for you to say," about our all-too-quickly-offered solutions? If you did, you were too respectful to say so. Instead, you put up with us and trudged ahead, trying this nostrum and that discipline until, despairing of them all, you cried uncle. Your fans in the stands cheered you on, convinced your tomorrow would be golden. You couldn't envision tomorrow; today was bathed in darkness and the darkness overcame the light.

> *I don't want any stupid blaming of yourself. As you well know I do my own thing with minimal adherence to counsel. Besides, if none of you is a closet psychic healer, there's not a thing to be done. I can't just take up space on this planet. I require a contribution of myself. Since none is forthcoming . . .*

For your dad, this is the worst paragraph in the letter. Not the part about not blaming ourselves. I've studied enough about grief and have walked with enough people through their losses to understand that mourning seldom moves in without self-blame taking over. When a loved one dies, your friends and family may exonerate you. They tell you there was nothing you could do to prevent the death, or that you did everything that could be done, or that your son knew what he was doing and even though he knew help was on the way he went ahead with his decision. So don't blame yourself.

That's what they say.

Like every other bereaved person I've known, my mind hears but can't quite believe. My eyes read your words, but my guilt isn't eased. I keep thinking of that morbid cartoon I saw some time ago, a picture of the cemetery headstone etched with the words, "I told you I was sick." Here's where my conscience accuses. I did know you were sick. I just didn't know how sick. Or what else I should have been doing to help you.

Fathers are fixers, you know. All your life, whenever you had problems, I wanted to solve them for you, to run interference, to ease the way. Then I'd catch myself, rein my impulses in, withdraw enough to protect you from my advice (which must often have seemed like scolding), encourage you to take off on your own. Did you know how to read my mixed signals? Did my love, struggling to find the proper distance, seem too aloof, too unpredictable? Were you reluctant to let me help because you were afraid I might take over? Or that I wouldn't? Or would disapprove?

Not that you gave me a hint of any of this. You came home as often as you could and stayed as long as you could. You seemed glad to be around and eager to talk when you felt up to it. We looked forward to every holiday. At Christmas we wouldn't put up the tree until you arrived. It just wouldn't have seemed right to go ahead without you. Besides, you were more adept at these things than your all-thumbs father.

It isn't because of you I've been blaming me. I suppose I still want to fix things, or better yet, to *have* fixed things so that this disaster would not have happened.

There is a little comfort—precious little—in your admission that you weren't particularly good at taking counsel. In this you were like every other twenty-something. It's the curse of the generation. I'm glad you weren't around to observe my own bull-headedness in those days (it's bad enough that you saw it in your father as you were growing up at home). What grace my parents and parents-in-law had to grant then, when I had so much to prove and was so determined to do it—whatever *it* was—*my* way. And what can I say of your longsuffering mother, who stayed with me when she must often have been scared or exasperated (or both) almost beyond endurance?

Obviously, I knew you didn't want a lot of advice from the older generation, just as I hadn't. Besides, I was proud of your attempts to make your own way. I think you knew that. And anyway, my biggest concern isn't with the advice I did or didn't subject you to. I agree with the counsel for fathers that I read a long time ago, advising us not to worry that our children aren't listening to us. There's a bigger worry: that they're always watching us. That resonated with me. I was middle-aged when I first ran across that truth. It made me realize that I had never stopped watching my own father. I started paying attention when I was a child. I was still carefully studying him in his old age, still seeking to learn from him (without asking, of course) how to be a man, a father, even later, a grandfather. You didn't need my advice; you needed a reliable role model. Scary thought.

> *I can't just take up space on this planet. I require a contribution of myself. Since none is forthcoming . . .*

Although you can excuse me for everything else, you can't let me off the hook here. I know where you learned this value. I hear my own voice teaching it in a sermon, in many sermons over many years. You heard my words. Even when you didn't seem to be listening, they hit home.

How I wish I could sit down with you and go over the lesson one more time, to tell you, "But that's not what I meant, not what I meant at all." I probably would have quoted Mark Twain's quip instead of an appropriate verse from the Bible, since quoting scripture in the moment would have struck you as predictably ministerial of me. "Let us endeavor so to live," he said, "that when we come to die even the undertaker will be sorry." Then I'd have then done my best to prove you had far surpassed Twain's standard.

How do you measure a contribution? What were you demanding of yourself? What did you think we desired for you? We made it clear we didn't expect you to follow in your father's footsteps. As a matter of fact, you made that pretty clear yourself. Remember how you used to answer people when they asked you if you were going to be a minister like your father? "No way," you'd emphatically tell them, and when we asked you why you felt so strongly about it, your answer was always the same: "I couldn't stand the hassles."

That always bewildered me. Ours has been a relatively hassle-free series of ministries. We haven't taken the beatings a lot of pastors and their families endure, never been fired, never missed a meal. As a matter of fact, we've considered ourselves spoiled by our churches. We've enjoyed a higher standard of living than your mother and I ever anticipated when we started life together. And our church leaders have for the most part been supportive.

We felt appreciated and even loved by our congregations. Central Christian Church in Mesa, for example, was remarkable. When your mother's health demanded we move, they let us make our home in Payson, eighty miles from the church, where the air was purer. She noticeably improved in the mountains, away from the Valley of the Sun's air pollution. Just two years later, when Pacific Christian College asked me to become president, for nine years they let me be president of a college in California while still maintaining the pastorate in Arizona. See what I mean, spoiled?

Through all our years in ministry, you didn't hear us complaining about our members at the dinner table or bemoaning our ill treatment—because we had so little to complain about. What "hassles" did you see that I couldn't see? The long hours, undoubtedly, but as you got older you caught on that they were more my fault than the churches'. I've never been very good at sitting. You, on the other hand, were a little more like your maternal grandfather, whom you loved so much. When the Whitneys moved to Tennessee to be closer to us, Grandpa Whitney used to talk about how much he liked practicing his "porch sittin'" there. He got good at it! It's an art I never mastered.

I'm wandering. We never expected my life choices to become yours. Your contribution didn't have to be measured in long hours on the job or certain academic pursuits. We were a little disappointed when you dropped out of college, but we understood. That illness again. It must have bothered you more than you let on. You had such a delightful mind. I know you felt cheated because it wasn't always reliable. That "fuzzy brain."

My sermons were crammed with stewardship principles. "God has given you everything—what are you doing for God?" I asked repeatedly. "How are you using your money to help people and serve God? Your time? Your talents? Your influence? What are you good for, for heaven's sake? And others' sake? Who is benefiting from you?" And on and on and on. I believe the right answer to these questions is critical for a fulfilling Christian life. But I've become afraid of my own preaching now, if these words can be used against a life as valuable, as irreplaceable, as yours.

Every autumn I used to preach for Pacific Christian College's[1] opening convocation. The fall semester after your death in May was very hard. I looked out at the sea of young, expectant faces and in every one of them I saw you. I hope you don't mind, but I told them about your letter. More specifically, I repeated what you said about making a contribution, about not just taking up space on the planet. I even told them how I longed to be able to have just one more talk with you, to assure you that you misunderstood me—or you understood me but undervalued your contribution.

I spoke as one under compulsion. I urged the students to accept God's acceptance of them. I wanted them to understand that in God's eyes they have eternal significance. Their assignment in college was to enhance their skills in order to serve effectively in the future. But in the meantime, right now, they are also making a contribution by being who they are. They are, each of them, unique, irreplaceable, young men and women of incalculable worth. They probably didn't fully grasp what I was driving at. Once again I could wish for another chance to make myself clear. It was a sermon preached more for the preacher—and the preacher's son—than for that assembled congregation, I'm afraid. They got the words I meant for you.

As I said, to your loved ones you were precious beyond calculation, your contribution to our lives irreplaceable. You were treasured for who you were, not for the measurable things you did. Without you we are less than we were.

That's it. That's the greatest contribution of all, isn't it? You made us more than we could be without you. You enhanced our lives—not just your family's, but your friends' as well. In your

1. Now renamed Hope International University.

presence they and we became more because of what you did for and to and through us. When you died and we all cried, the tears were for our loss. Do you get it? We have all *lost* you and feel ourselves to be lessened because we no longer have you. What else is this but *contribution*?

Your letter implies we would be better off without you, without the worry. Wrong. Oh, how wrong.

Remember how you grieved when your crazy companion Sylva, that irrepressible canine of uncertain parentage, died? I'm wondering what contribution you thought Sylva was making to the betterment of this world. She took up considerable space for a pet, didn't she? And what a bother! Yet when you brought Sylva home with you, we saw to what selfless lengths you went to make certain your dog's every need was met and that she didn't feel slighted when she couldn't come into the house because of your father's allergies. You were, it seemed to me, equally solicitous of dog and Dad. We both appreciated it.

Then she died, and your grief was deep. I ask again, what contribution did she make? She enhanced you, that's what she did. She gave you a reason to earn, to give, to work, and to want to come home from work. She couldn't even talk to you, but she could listen and communicate in her own way. She trusted you. She affirmed you. She loved you. And you loved her. You were a better person because she was in your life.

Is any further contribution required?

I know, I know, you're going to protest that she's a dog and therefore nothing more is required. She's a dog and you're a man, so this is different. You probably want to preach me another of my sermons, "Of whom much is given, much is required." True. But did you hear any of my attempts to describe the grace of God, that undeserved favor which God bestows on us even though we think we are unworthy? Did you catch on to my Bible-based insistence that salvation is by faith and grace, not by works and merit?

As you can see, I'm feeling defensive here. I think I blew it— and I don't know how to keep from blowing it again. Just let me tell you one more time how great was your contribution to my life. Since you've been gone, I've been almost afraid to preach. I don't want to unwittingly hang another heavy load of guilt on the innocent. Yet there are some things that the preacher must say. Sin controls and confuses; its devilish powers cannot be brushed aside. Unfortunately, the tender take what they hear too personally, as if I'm speaking only to them; the calloused assume I'm talking about someone else. So what shall I say, how shall I say it, how can I be certain no one else ever fatally misunderstands?

I'm aware you won't approve of this breast-beating. You'll tell me I'm attaching too much importance to my sermons and that you didn't get this idea from them. As always, you'd be sensitive to my feelings. And you may not have got the idea from me. But what eats at my soul is that you very well could have, because I've preached it enough. Thanks, though, for accepting the responsibility. It helps. Some.

One more thought. From somewhere back in the distant days of my early education (was it in high school or college?) comes some required memory work. The assignment stuck. We were studying *Macbeth*. The quotation is Macbeth's response on just learning of his wife's death. These are some of Shakespeare's most famous lines. I wonder now whether our instructor thought Macbeth was telling the truth. I hope not.

> "Out, out, brief candle!
> Life's but a walking shadow, a poor player
> That struts and frets his hour upon the stage,
> And then is heard no more; it is a tale
> Told by an idiot, full of sound and fury,
> Signifying nothing."

Memorable words, admittedly, but so, so far from the truth. "Idiot" is Macbeth's description. "Wuss" is your self-description. Just as far from reality.

As I revise yet again this ongoing conversation, it's startling to realize it's been almost thirty years now since you left us. Your contribution shines ever more brightly with the passing of the years and your importance to your loved ones remains as compelling as ever. Your role on the stage is anything but strutting and fretting. It signified so much!

It still does.

> *I'm also curious about what's next. It's got to be better than this, but I won't know till I'm there. I hope there's no afterlife or reincarnation, because I'm ready to just be dead. Geez, just writing this is making my shoulder burn.*

Here's a paragraph to make a preacher cry. Or boast. I don't know where you got the idea of reincarnation. In our conversations about religion, you didn't introduce this topic. After you were gone, we were told that one of your friends (was it your roommate Jeff?) was a strong believer in the transmigration of souls through various incarnations and that he had been pushing his belief on you, but you weren't buying.

Apparently, you weren't buying orthodox Christianity's teaching regarding heaven, either. Does it seem like too easy an escape? Too much like "pie in the sky by and by"? You were determined to accept nothing except on evidence and you weren't satisfied with the traditional proofs of Christian apologists. On the other hand, in one of our talks you were honest enough to admit you hadn't investigated your own Christian heritage with the same scrutiny you applied to others.

You are clear: you wouldn't indulge in any life after death "fantasies" even in your final letter. You were seeking oblivion, not reincarnation or resurrection.

Your words took me back once more to my own twenties. Like you, I wasn't having any trouble listening to preaching and teaching about Jesus. It made sense that, if there were a creator of this world, he would seek some means of communicating with his creation, some way of making himself known. Thus Jesus. Many of the trappings of formalized religion, however, gave me intellectual heartburn.

So did some of the teachings, among them traditional doctrines of heaven and hell. When I learned, for example, that the Israelites did not as a rule believe in life after death, that it appeared in Jewish faith only a few generations before Christ and that it was still a debated issue in Jesus' day between the Sadducees and Pharisees, I was intrigued. It seemed strange that such a vital doctrine should have somehow evolved in Jewish consciousness and not be a "thus sayeth the Lord" from the beginning.

And what evidence is there yet? Jesus' teaching, and that of Paul, primarily. The apostles' testimony to the resurrection of their master. The witness of up to five hundred who saw Jesus alive, according to Paul in 1 Corinthians 15. Yet a skeptic could object—skeptics *have* objected—that these so-called proofs fail the test of empirical evidence because they all come from one source, the New Testament. What evidence have non-believers found? What substantial case has science offered?

Eventually I came around, accepting on faith the testimony of scripture. I would have to take the Bible's word for it and wait, like you, to see what's next after death. For the most part I've been satisfied with this position, trying my best to discern and obey God's will for my life now and place my future in God's hands. I guess I'm kind of like Mark Twain, who said, "It ain't those parts of the Bible that I can't understand that bother me, it is the parts that I do understand."

I can't find "scientific" proof that there is more to life than what this body of flesh holds; neither can I scientifically prove there isn't. Since adequate scientific evidence is lacking either way, I choose to believe the scriptures that when I die there is still more to come, as there has been for you. But I will live every day I have now to the fullest so that, when it is over, I will not have substituted wishful thinking for living, something then for nothing now.

Wise old Charles Thomas, an elder in my home church, gave me this insight in my high school days. I sought the advice of this thoroughly good man more than once back then. Interesting—I turned to him during a period when I had a typical teenager's distrust of parental advice. It didn't strike me then as a little ironic that I wanted Charley's take on things. Charley was the same man my dad listened to when he needed some guidance! On this subject of life after death, Charley said he had concluded that, as Pascal had

27

recommended, a leap of faith was called for, a genuine "bet your life." I should add that Charley had never read Pascal.

So much of the best advice I've received through the years has come from "the unlettered," ordinary folks, not scholars. Charley bet his life on God and looked forward to heaven. This was his stance, he explained, because "either way I win. If there is a heaven and I'm prepared for it, I win. If there isn't, I still win, because as a Christian I will have lived the best possible kind of life here."

I placed the same bet.

You weren't ready yet. You were still probing, checking out the probabilities, exploring the alternatives. If I had felt as rotten as you did at the end, I undoubtedly would have wanted what you wanted: just let it be over!

Once more Dianne gave us encouragement. The fact that you chose her, a believer, as your best friend says something about where you were religiously. Dianne told us of some of your conversations. She was convinced you were returning to the faith you were taught, only now it would be your choice, not something you merely inherited. We're hanging on to her words.

> *Don't be sad for me. This is what I most need. Don't grieve too long for yourselves, get on with your life. Raise an occasional glass of wine or beer (my personal recommendation is the Mouton Cadet Cabernet Sauvignon) to my memory, and strive to be happy since I couldn't.*

Two impossible requests: "*Don't be sad for me . . . don't grieve too long for yourselves.*" The third we have had to do, of course: "*Get on with your life.*" The fourth we obeyed, but in a way you wouldn't have guessed.

In your truck was the unopened bottle of the Mouton Cadet Cabernet Sauvignon you recommended. We put it to good use. After the formal memorial service at Brookings Christian Church, we drove up the coast to Port Orford for a private family communion service at The Rock. We all agreed this was the proper place. Your grandparents had bought the adjacent small acreage before you were born. They later expanded it to the five acres you knew so well, with its 163-foot beach frontage and—just to the south of the property, right at the shoreline—one of the large haystack rocks for which the Oregon coast is famous. You played there as a child, splashing in the ocean-fed puddles, collecting the hermit crabs and anemones and starfish, lost in the many-splendored wonders of the seashore; you returned there as an adult, more at home there than almost anywhere else you'd lived. It just seemed right to us, then, to make our own way, as if on spiritual pilgrimage, to The Rock for this holy moment.

Family goes to The Rock for the last service.

As we expected, a vigorous wind was ramming the ocean breakers against the rock ledge at the base of The Rock, the air glistening with spray. Sunbeams pierced the clouds, mist refracted the rays. It was, despite the awfulness of the occasion, awesome. Your sister Candy sang for us; your Velcro brother Brian accompanied on his guitar.

Then came our private Communion service, each of us quiet, immersed in our private thoughts of you, meditating. Grandpa Whitney prayed, and we partook of the bread and, yes, your wine.

Brian and Jeff did not, because of the alcoholism in their families. We had found some cranberry juice in your kitchen cupboard, so they drank this substitute. It was still yours. I smiled a bit at what you might have said as you observed your generally teetotaling family (yes, your mother and your grandparents, too) tasting wine because it was *yours*. Because you had asked. Because it was a way of somehow reaching you, of communing with you. It was not exactly the party spirit you recommended, but it brought us a kind of subdued joy, as communion of souls always does.

You would relish the irony of this, that the self-proclaimed prodigal son brought to the loving father a new insight into this simple Christian rite, one your mother and I have observed weekly since childhood. I've often brought our church's attention to the fact that, when meeting at the Lord's Table, we are linked with Christians all over the globe. At The Rock we added a dimension. We were reaching beyond space into time, grasping not only the hand of the Lord here and now, but also your hand already in the time to come. "Neither height nor depth, neither death nor life . . . can separate us . . ." (Romans 8:39)

Our communion at The Rock reminded me of the Christmas you missed. You were an exchange student in Germany that year, your seventeenth. We'd never had a holiday without all of us together before; we weren't looking forward to this one, since Christmas was our favorite time of the year. We were dreading your absence, but you came to our rescue. You sent your journal from Germany as our Christmas present. A perfect choice. It arrived just in time, so after we finished opening presents, we lingered in the living room, immediate and Velcro ("unofficially adopted") family together, and for the next hour or two I read your journal aloud. We laughed and cried and remembered. No one wanted to leave. You had never been more present than you were the Christmas you were absent.

So it was at The Rock.

After the service I walked to The Rock's edge, where the breakers were pounding and the wind was so powerful I had to brace myself against it. There I did something more difficult than anything else I can remember. With the family looking on, I cast your ashes into the wind and the waves.

The party was over.

When your mother reread this manuscript a final time she said, "No, the party wasn't over." She reminded me that as we stood at the water's edge, three seals suddenly appeared in the water in front of us, just yards out from The Rock, cavorting playfully as if putting on a show for our benefit, almost close enough for us to touch them, as if oblivious to the heaviness in our hearts, as if offering their mute but eloquent tribute to your own playfulness, your typical zest for life. God didn't send us a rainbow. God sent us seals—to remind us of our hope.

> *More practical thoughts keep coming to mind, so I'd better get them out of the way. Regarding my funeral, I want the least amount spent as possible. Plain wood box. Smallest possible (6" by 6" is what comes to mind) inscribed "Bozo to the end." No funeral parlor. No rehashing my little life, boiling it down to it's meaningless essence. Just say a few words and drop me in the cheapest plot available. If it is cheaper to have me cremated and toss my ashes. Who wants a morbid urn hanging around? I want my death like my life; short, to the point, minimalist, and humorous if you can manage.*

You were cremated, but not because it was cheaper than burial. As soon as we thought of The Rock, we knew we had no choice. That's where you belonged.

Because you died on Thursday night before Memorial Day weekend, and because your death was by suicide, we couldn't make arrangements quickly. The sheriff's office held your body until Tuesday. They had to be satisfied there was no foul play. Then we had to get the coroner's clearance before the body could be released to a funeral director. So from Friday morning, when two policemen woke your mother at 4:00 AM in Payson with the terrible news, until the services on Wednesday, we had plenty of time to decide how to honor your wishes. It would be cremation. Your ashes would be scattered on the ocean. We briefly considered taking a boat farther offshore for the ceremony, but that thought was quickly overruled; we wanted to connect you forever with The Rock.

This solved another problem. There was no way on earth we could have any kind of headstone with "Bozo to the end" on it. This little attempt at humor failed, Son. The audience wasn't laughing. Try as you might, you never pulled off the Bozo act. We would laugh along with your self-directed put-downs when you were around, because you knew and we knew that you were anything but a clown. A wit, for sure. A charmer, beyond a doubt. A purveyor of laughter and gaiety, always. A Bozo, never.

As you requested, no funeral parlor. We asked Pastor Keith Sorenson of the Christian Church in Brookings, a ministerial colleague, for permission to hold a small family service there on Wednesday morning. Not only did he agree, but the church then went into action to help us. (A well-known pastor once commented that he had long thought what people do best is funerals, which elicit their sense of protocol, their wisdom, and their caring hearts. He was right.) We didn't know until we arrived that this was your girlfriend's church, so they were assisting for her sake as well as for yours and ours. Among other kind acts, they plastered the wall with cards your friends and ours had sent in your memory.

We intended to keep it very simple. Mom and I didn't even call our extended families, wanting to spare them the complications of taking off work and making the difficult drive to Brookings, a remote location. We have always been confident of their love and concern; that was enough. In retrospect, I wish they could have joined us to learn firsthand what we heard about you, and to share the experience with us. It was not a good decision.

This one was: Disregarding your instructions, we did rehash your life. We had to boil your story down—there was so much to tell—but the real you came through. The quiet family gathering we had planned turned into a large congregation. Your friends in Brookings, unaware we had prepared a memorial service, were putting their own together. They had invited the town. They graciously scrapped their plans and participated in ours. That meant a fairly long session—you wouldn't have approved—with all our family who could talk taking part along with Jon, your *tai chi* instructor; Jeff, your roommate; and Lori from the martial arts club. If you wouldn't have been so peeved at us for doing this in the first place, the many tributes would have touched you.

And you'd have laughed at Brian. Ever since that week, we've been calling *him* a "rock." Before we left Mesa, he was already earning this nickname. He rushed to our condo as soon as Judy, my administrative assistant, told him he had to get ahold of us. She wouldn't tell him why. He arrived before anyone else except Roland and Phyllis Lee. These best-of-friends had driven your mother down the mountain from Payson—they didn't want her to drive by herself—so she could deliver the bad news in person rather than on the phone. I had just arrived from California the night before. Brian hadn't been with us in the condo long when the phone rang. He answered, thinking he could best help by taking over the phone duties. "Hello," he said.

"Brian?" It was Don Cox, one of our pastors. That did it. Brian choked up, couldn't speak, and handed me the phone.

Then at your service he was one of the speakers. He tried to read the scripture as a part of his remarks, but he choked up again, and finally he asked me to come to the pulpit and finish reading for him. A great help!

Actually, he was. His love for you was transparent, and his temporary muteness spoke volumes. Our ability to laugh together about his "performance" afterward continued to ease the tension.

Back to your letter. Some things you just can't direct, Son. You can live, you can even take your life, but you are powerless to dictate its long-term effect on others. Your life was short but not minimalist. You lived too big, you touched too many of us too deeply, for your abrupt departure to be insignificant.

We did manage some humor. You helped us with that. We just had to recall the little boy who called himself "a problem drinker" (when you spilled your milkshake in the back seat of the car), the young man who hated to wear shoes, the birthday and Christmas presents you wrapped with such peerless imperfection, the boyfriend who faced the cop's gun when he was innocently talking with his girlfriend through her open bedroom window one midnight, . . . and on and on went the stories we told each other, laughing. And then crying.

Your life was short. Your impact was forever.

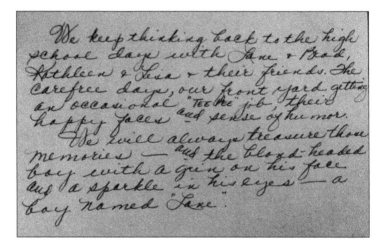

The note the parents of Lane's high school girlfriend sent to his parents

Sell off my stuff to pay for it. I would like my radio and music to go Dianne. I'd also like her to get at least a grand ($1,000) if my "estate" can do that. You may not know it, but she is the love of my life. I'm sorry for the unsurmountable obstacles between us, and that we got together when I'd had it. She's an incredibly wonderful person, one of the best I've ever known. She gets whatever she wants of my stuff. The antiques at the store are mine, so keep what you want and sell the rest. Try to cash the AT&T check that will come shortly to give to Dianne. The piano goes to Albert Williams my piano teacher. Leave my finances in the ruin I left them, and use my stuff for a little fun yourselves.

No, we didn't know about Dianne. Your sister Candy thought maybe you were not telling us about her because you were afraid we might not approve, since she was several years older than you.

We doubt this was the reason, because, as you knew so well, we had approved of the other girlfriends you had chosen over the years. As a matter of fact, we can't think of any friend, male or female, we disapproved of. Like your parents and sisters, you seemed to like variety. You were never a snob. What you did require was authenticity. Posturing was not your style and you didn't like it in friends.

When we met Dianne we felt we were receiving your last gift to us. The day we arrived at the county courthouse in Gold Beach to start the prolonged process of claiming your body, someone passed on her message. She wanted to meet us. We spent a few hours together, including lunch. It was at that table I realized how much she was like your mother. A classy lady. Like you, we wish she had come into your life (and ours) sooner. The more we learned of her the better we liked her.

You can imagine our delight in discovering her Christian belief and learning from her of the long talks you two had about the meaning of faith. I wish I could have listened in. I'd have been a little envious. You would have talked to her with a candor that is hard to manage with one's father, especially when he's a pastor and you're not wanting to openly challenge his beliefs.

Even though we knew how badly she needed the financial help, we reluctantly did as she insisted with money you wanted her to have. She simply would not benefit materially from your death. Later, we were able to convince her to receive a little gift from us. We felt compelled to do something, even though our something was less than you wanted for her. The next Easter we persuaded her to accept a ticket to fly to Mesa to spend a few days with us. We were being selfish, we admit. We wanted to get to know her better and to learn all we could about your life in Brookings. We were hoping to hang on to her for a lifetime.

I'm afraid we failed you on the antiques. Your former business partner turned out to be less than kind. I've already groused enough about her. Well, maybe a little more is permissible. Her denial that the antiques even existed was a huge disappointment to your mother, with her love of antiques *and* her son, especially of antiques that were her son's. Even the trunk you and she refinished together, back when you were setting up the shop, was gone. Our parting was less than amicable. We haven't seen her since.

A word about your monthly disability check. We cashed it, as I said. Later, I had to send a check to reimburse the company for the few days from May 26 to the end of the month. They were not about to let your estate receive money you weren't alive to "earn." Not a word of condolence, not an offer to help with funeral expenses. Just: Send us what you owe us. Period. So much for the heart of big business.

It was a real pleasure to give Mr. Williams the piano as you instructed and to distribute the few personal items the family selected. The "Thing" went to six Whitney boys, your cousins. I was particularly proud to display your sword and sash on my office wall. Your mother arranged them along with a favorite picture of you teaching a class of children. It's proof that I was right. I had long been convinced you were meant to be a teacher! But this memorial had to come down. It was too easy to glance up from my desk to that wall. The photo and memorabilia fixed my mind all over again on how much I had lost. That glance reopened the wound—every day. It was more than I could bear. I needed more time to heal.

Lane teaching children tai chi

I love my family, greatest people on Earth,
sorry I couldn't hang with you longer.

Of your love for your family we've never had a doubt. Thanks for telling us one last time, though.

Well, I went back down and sent some money to Dianne.
And a message to come look for my body. Terrible way to
do it, but I wanted to make sure she got the moola and

that I was found before I rotted too much. I also had a pretty good last meal, all the things I'm not supposed to eat. Didn't come up with a reason not to go through with this, so here I am again.

In spite of the anguish we felt as we read your letter, this paragraph made us smile. "All the things I'm not supposed to eat." For the better part of twenty years your diet was a challenge. I remembered when your mother pressed the Feingold Diet on you, which banned many of your favorite foods. I reminisced again about the small boy who couldn't drink anything but water because everything else seemed to attack his stomach. The natural food period, the vegetarian period, the almost-nothing-but-rice period. No tomatoes, no apples, nothing containing food coloring, no candy, no, no, no, no. Each diet promised relief but inevitably disappointed.

Then one last meal. Savoring, swallowing, taking your revenge, as if you were defying your body: "Serves you right. Take that. And that."

But then the smile fades. Here's proof we didn't want. On Tuesday, between your first attempt on Monday and your success on Thursday, you phoned home. Your words were filled with assurance for your fretting parents. "Don't worry." Mom confirmed her new flight's arrival time. She told you Dr. Nichols was mailing you some anti-depressant medicine. You knew help was on the way.

You didn't want it. No "reason not to go through with this."

There is probably more to the story than either you or we knew at the time. In recent years doctors have learned a great deal about Lyme disease, particularly one of its symptoms, severe depression. When you first moved to Oregon, you stayed for several months in Grandpa Whitney's tiny cabin in Port Orford. Without electricity or plumbing, this ten-by-twelve-foot structure was nestled in the dense woods and underbrush, a breeding ground for contemplative thoughts—and ticks. You were bitten by a Lyme-carrying insect and, suspicious, you were taking medicine for it. In those day, though, depression was not yet associated with the disease. We can't keep from charging it, at least in part, for your fatal decision.

Lane's grandpa built this cabin in the 1950s. Lane retreated to it in the 1990s, trying to regain his health.

Some more questions.

Why before Hawaii? I figured I'd just spend the money someone else could use. I'd be consumed by the thoughts of doing this all the while, so I wouldn't really enjoy myself. Besides, I woke up this morning so bad off I really don't care. No time like the present, eh?

This section of your letter is so typically Lawson! We're great explainers. We concoct convincing arguments (persuasive to us, at least) that appear reasonable, especially when we're not being reasonable. Your explanations contain a kernel of logic, I have to admit, but only a kernel.

You had your heart set on a brief vacation trip to Hawaii. Your last-minute cancellation surprised us. We had sent you a frequent flyer coupon so you could fly for free. You upgraded it to first class ("He can afford an upgrade to first class?" mused your frugal father.) Well, first-class to Hawaii we could understand. Not going at all, ever—that's harder to take in. Your sister Candy eventually went in your place. The Lawson frugality insists that a ticket should not be wasted.

> *Why not wait for antidepressants? I don't like 'em, and they wouldn't stop the pain. I don't figure the yeast stuff is really going to help either. Better to just let someone who wants to live fill the gap I leave.*

This deals with a question that tormented us on our flight from Phoenix to Portland and the drive down the southern Oregon coast to Brookings. Why not wait for the help from your mother's visit and for the medicine to kick in?

We knew you didn't like medications. You never had. In our opinion, you did not give them a fair chance. You were too impatient, wouldn't wait for their effect. Whether it was legitimate medicine or homespun remedies, you'd try them for a while, then quit. Prozac, for example. Mom had begun taking it some months earlier. She required only a small amount, less than the normally prescribed dose. But these days, when people ask what is responsible for her improved health, while she usually gives credit to the mounds of herbs and various supplements she takes, I always mention Prozac, because it was when she began taking it—after the usual six weeks required for its effect—that she showed remarkable improvement. I was almost afraid to mention the change I saw in her; I didn't want to "spook" the treatment. We were so glad you agreed to try the medicine, and then were deeply dismayed when, after just a few days, you discarded it. We still wonder whether, if you'd just been a little more patient. . . .

> *Better to just let someone who wants to fill the gap I leave.*

But who could? Now I'm baffled again. Surely you didn't believe anyone could take your place in our hearts, as if our children were like interchangeable parts. Is one missing? Oh well, just move another one over into his slot. This isn't reason talking, it's rationalization—no, even that word gives it more respect than it deserves. It's depression, dark feelings, reason's capitulation, despair trampling hope in the dust. Against such determined loss of will to live, logic is helpless.

If I love you, why? Would you really rather I lived like this?
Better to put your worries at rest also.

A hard question, yielding no acceptable response. I've already said it often. We have never doubted your love. We have also never doubted that love was your motive, or at least one of your motives. And no, we wouldn't choose for you to live as you were living. Neither would we choose for you not to live.

Were these the only two viable options? We saw a third. We thought healing was possible. We had experienced your mother's dramatic improvement. Her struggle went on for many years, also, but she was much, much better in 1994 than she was in 1988, when we moved to Payson in her quest to find cleaner air. By then her dogged search for better health had driven her to many dead ends. She bore the stigma of the misunderstood, charged as a natural food fanatic, a neurotic, a hypochondriac tramping from doctor to doctor seeking a cure for some elusive and, most of them decided, probably merely psychosomatic illness.

She also endured the well-meaning but bothersome hordes of persons who pestered her with their favorite panaceas. Each was convinced he or more often she had *the* cure for what ailed her. None had any idea how many others had foisted their fool-proof elixirs on her. She tried many, to her inevitable disappointment. Yet she persisted. And eventually succeeded.

She was so stubborn because the health of three was at stake. She was the self-appointed pioneer, the guinea pig, a harried mother scrambling to save her little ones. If she could find relief for herself, she reasoned, maybe she could give some hope to you and your sister. Her advantage was her age. By the time you're fifty, you have mellowed out a bit, acquired some patience. At twenty-six, you're in a hurry, seeking the quick fix, convinced that what life has thrown at you so far is likely as good as it gets. "No time like the present," you say, expecting us to agree with you. Well, we don't. At our age, we've accepted that no two days are alike, that what is now is not what's going to be; it's certainly not as good as it gets. Life is flux, unpredictability. Things may get better or they may get worse, but you can bet on it: they aren't going to stay the same.

No, we wouldn't have condemned you to live the way you were living indefinitely. We would have done everything we could to help you, to persuade you to hope, because we absolutely wanted you to live.

You knew that, of course. When you'd phone home or we'd call, you and I would chat about a few things and then I'd bow out so your mother and you could compare health notes. "Have you tried this?" she would ask. "Have I told you how much help I'm getting from . . . ?" You listened with respectful tolerance, polite but—it is now so apparent—unconvinced. Yet one fact surely had to have impressed you: she was improving. And she was sure you could, too.

No, we wouldn't have wanted you to continue as you were. But oh, how we wanted you to continue!

Why here?

I like this campground. Plus I figured I won't be stopped here, and I'll be found soon enough. It's nice and shady so my body won't get to hot and get nasty.

After your teacher Jon led the family to the campground, we applauded your choice of venue, even though we deplored your performance. This is a place of breathtaking beauty, with its towering Douglas fir trees, its soft carpet of needles, its scintillating dance of sunlight and shadows (on a clear, non-rainy Oregon day, of course). You and your friends often camped here, we were told. Not far from town, yet the place seems remote, pristine, safely protected from human exploitation. Nature as God designed it. Peaceful, so peaceful.

You were right, too, about your friends knowing where to look for you. When you were discovered missing, Jon drove directly to this site. Your truck's engine was still running.

Close, but too late.

Why this way?

I was going to use the gun, but that's pretty gross to find. Believe it or not I'm trying to be as thoughtful as this sort of thing allows.

Thanks for trying, Son. Death by asphyxiation is pretty gross, also.

> *Enough writing. Again, I'm really sorry. Please forgive me. Have a great life. I'm on to better things, so don't worry about me. No more pain, yeah!*

We forgave you before you asked. We forgave you when you and your sisters were teenagers and your mother and I faced the stark possibility that we could outlive at least one of our children. We were up against an enemy we could not defeat. The Bible says our battle "is not against flesh and blood but against principalities and powers in the heavenly places." In your case, though, the battle in the beginning *was* against flesh and blood, and we didn't hold the weapon that could defeat it. We couldn't foresee our children's future. We only knew that nothing you could or would do or that would be done to you could separate us from our love for you. Then, in the end, the "principalities and powers" won.

> *I'm on to better things . . .*

We believe that. We hope you believed that, too.

And there is some comfort in knowing you don't hurt any more.

> *I love you,*
>
> *Lane*

I love you too, Son. I always will. I just hope I told you often enough.

Oh, what I'd give to be able to tell you so now.

III

REFLECTIONS

1

Faith Is Not Inheritable

"I have been reminded of your sincere faith,
which first lived in your

grandmother Lois and in your mother
Eunice and, I am persuaded,

now lives in you also."

2 Timothy 1:5

A FEW QUESTIONS FOR this preacher: Just how do you hand your faith on to your children? You can't claim much success for yourself, can you? What advice, then, can you give to other believing parents?

We raised three children. One, our firstborn, is a believer, an active member of a church along with her husband, Ed. All Kim's life she sought, like the stereotypical firstborn, to please her parents. She succeeded. She is a loving, solicitous daughter (and an inspiring mother and grandmother), but she has never been anybody's puppet. Always independent, assertive, and resourceful (she established and successfully operated her own business), she isn't afraid to challenge authority figures when she doubts them and won't accept anything from anybody (including her father) just because they say so. Her faith, though it has much in common with her parents', is *her* faith.

Candace, the second child, also fits a stereotype in several ways, including her disapproval of my categorizing her in this way. Candy was restless, sometimes rebellious. As a child she quickly discerned that her older sister had filled the "compliant child" slot, so she sought attention by other means. But she has also always been loving, intuitive, expressive, very bright—and a whole lot of fun. At one time I'd have said she rejected her parents' faith and teaching. At times, I confess, it felt as if she had rejected me as well. She always insisted, I'm gratified to say, I read her wrong. I was too wrapped up in my own ego. More than once she remonstrated, "Now Dad, don't take this as rejection." She was telling the truth. It wasn't rejection. It was curiosity, personal growth, the need to be herself. One of the unanticipated pleasures of my old age is that Candy and I now enjoy open, mutually respectful explorations of spiritual subjects, the kind I'm confident you and I would be having if only. . . .

You were the lastborn, Lane, the only son, everybody's friend. I'm uncertain when you began to doubt. There were signs when you were a teenager. Your Velcro brother Brian says he discerned your drifting "from the faith of the father" when you were in high school. In our conversations in your twenties, you confirmed Brian's suspicions.

Your doubts didn't alarm me. Maturation requires distancing, individuating. I announced as an adolescent to my probably disappointed father that I'd never be a grocer. Why? Because that's who *he* was. Case closed. Your mom told me on our first date she'd never marry a minister. (It's pretty obvious what her father was, isn't it?) For the Lawson kids, becoming your own persons meant coming to terms—your own terms—with religion.

The truth is, I've been proud of each of you for your independence of thought and your embrace of the Christian ethic, if not of all Christian dogma—with which, as you know, I have had some arguments myself.

I am talking about faith in this first reflection, I suppose, because I'm supposed to. I feel compelled to address this hazard of my profession, this general expectation that the pastor's children will obediently line up behind him in the march toward heaven. Some of my ministerial colleagues take justifiable pride in pointing out—even when no one is asking them to—how all their sons are preachers, all their daughters are preachers' wives, and of course all their grandchildren will follow suit. These are good people and I rejoice with them. I do admire them.

But I don't envy them. What I can boast of is that all you children have taken the faith so seriously you would not settle for spiritual hand-me-downs, even the opinions of your theologically educated, professionally accredited father, the one you loved to address (with a snicker) as "Reverend Professor Doctor Lawson, Sir" while at the same time not letting me get away with anything just because I said it was so.

There are, it has been said, no second-generation Christians. You can't get to heaven on your parents' coattails. You can't even claim any kind of spiritual superiority because your father or your grandfather was a minister, your mother or grandmother a saint, a real saint.

The real problem with parenthood, I have often lamented, is that you bring up your children to become independent adults.

And then you succeed.

I always utter this complaint with a smile.

2

Suicide Is Not an Unforgivable Sin

OUR FAITH, YOUR MOTHER's and mine, rests solidly on the New Testament. Thanks to these scriptures, we haven't been bedeviled by hellish visions of damnation, the destiny stored up for benighted souls who commit suicide. Such teaching is simply, in our opinion, heretical. Suicide is not the unforgivable sin, though belief that it is has tortured so many. They were taught that persons who take their own lives are playing God, with disastrous results. The reasoning goes something like this: by taking their lives into their own hands, people make it impossible to repent and ask God's forgiveness and receive God's grace. You can't repent after you're dead. Therefore, God can't forgive you. End of story.

For centuries no victim of suicide could be buried in a Christian cemetery. They died in sin and out of reach of redemption. Generation after generation of believers have agonized over this cruel tenet. Church dogma and ecclesiastical authority stood behind it. But scripture simply does not offer an explicit, "Thou shalt not commit suicide." The German philosopher Immanuel Kant captures our struggle to understand the mind of God on this issue: "Suicide is not abominable because God forbids it; God forbids it because it is abominable." Something so hateful to us, we reason, must be hateful to God. Therefore, God could not tolerate it, must have outlawed it.

But such reasoning pushes us into believing what the scriptures do not explicitly mandate.

I had to make my own study of the subject long before you died, Son. A minister can't escape this one. We have served large congregations; I've presided over many funerals—among them altogether too many for people who took their own lives. What could I say to bereaved families? What comfort could I offer, what hope? And for that matter, what did I personally really believe?

One thing for certain I could say: My ministerial ordination did not bestow the right or the insight to determine who is saved and who is lost. I am not qualified to judge. Nor, for that matter, is anyone else. Who can fully know the heart and mind of another person? In place of predicting the deceased's eternal destiny, I could instead draw on the grace of a God who knows the innermost workings of the heart—and cares. I had read that one in every four high school students had seriously thought about killing themselves in the previous year. I had counseled some of them both in the years I was a high school and college teacher and in my many years as a pastor. I *counseled*, offering comfort and hope. What I did not do was preach them into or out of heaven.

"To be or not to be, that is the question." Shakespeare's young Hamlet's dilemma has resonated through centuries because it rings true for so many. Some philosophers have argued that this is the *only* real question. Do I take my life or not? And if not, why not? When I was still young, the philosophical became very personal for me: Could I believe God would have permanently cast off my students or parishioners because in their despair they sought to end their lives? I couldn't. Then I had to deal with your own answer to Hamlet's question. "Not to be," you opted. The solace I offered so many other mourners in earlier years I now extended to my mourning self. And to our family. We simply didn't believe God would turn his back on you, in spite of your choice. That would be out of character for God.

I was wrong about one thing, though. I once bought into the common misconception that you didn't need to fret when someone threatened suicide. They didn't mean it, people said, especially when they threatened because a lover jilted them, or the promotion they expected didn't come through, or because they were just "getting even." They were bidding for attention or sympathy, people also said. This is just manipulation, they said. "If they're talking about it, they'll be all right. Not to worry," they said. Maybe, but probably not. Now I *always* take them seriously.

And while I'm confessing how much I have had to learn on the subject, here's another lesson: I used to trust someone who promised, after a botched attempt, "You don't have to worry about me. I learned my lesson. I won't try that again." Wrong. They may have been sincere in the moment, but then depression overwhelms them again. Their sincerity evaporates; they don't have the strength to resist.

The Lawson Family Illness has proved to us the destructive power of chemical imbalance. Overcoming depression, I once confidently asserted, was just a matter of "bucking up," of "applying some self-discipline," of "mind over matter," of practicing "the old stiff upper lip." And, you'd expect this from a pastor, of putting your faith into practice.

It's just not that simple.

I have had a lot of repenting to do.

Especially in your case, Son. I couldn't conceive that a member of *our* family, no matter how severe the illness, could commit suicide. We're "stronger than that." We are overcomers. There has never been a suicide in either your mother's family or mine, I consoled myself. Never has been, never will be.

Today, studying your picture, I still shake my head in disbelief. So confident, so winsome, so much the winner. No, yours is not the face of a suicidal person. You'll come through this ordeal. Of course. That's what our family does.

I had so much to learn. You taught me.

But even in the distress of those first hours after the police delivered the bad news, fighting to make sense of the inexplicable, we didn't compound our confusion and grief by worrying about your eternal destiny. Suicide would not separate you from God. It is not blasphemy against the Holy Spirit; it is not an irreversible rejection of your heavenly Father—or, for that matter, *by* Him, either. The Spirit "who searches our hearts" and "intercedes for us with groans that words cannot express" (Romans 8:26, 27) isn't called our Advocate without reason. You are in safe hands with God. God is on *your* side.

I love the apostle Paul's assurance just a few verses later (v. 31) "If God be for us, who can be against us?" OK, I'm on a roll. Paul didn't stop there and neither can I: "For I am persuaded, that neither death, nor life, nor angels, nor principalities, nor powers, nor things present, nor things to come, nor height, nor depth, nor any other creature, shall be able to separate us from the love of God, which is in Christ Jesus our Lord." See why I don't think suicide gets the last word?

Your death showed me something else. What I did not know before was how many of this pastor's flock had attempted suicide. When they learned of your death and our ordeal, it was as if some powerful key had unlocked their own secrets, their long-stifled anguish. They now felt safe in confessing their struggles to their pastor; they began treating my office as a confessional. They sent cards, wrote letters, scheduled appointments. They wanted Mom and me to hear what had led them to attempt it; they hoped, by relating their stories, to offer us a little more insight into why you did what you did. They sought to help us understand you—and themselves.

Others, whose loved ones had taken their lives, told us their stories as well. They hadn't fully recovered from their loss yet—and never would, they warned us—but they promised us that, as life has gone on for them, so it would for us. In time.

3

Why I Nearly Quit

IN THE FOLLOWING MONTHS, your death plunged me into near despair. It did the same to your mother and sisters. We mourned together and separately, seeking solace in each other while also needing space to heal in our individual ways. Predictably, I buried myself in work, surfacing occasionally to remember, reflect, and ache. Mom withdrew into quietness and solitude and the empathy of her support group of caregivers. She had joined them sometime earlier, seeking the advice and encouragement of other parents whose children suffered various types of mental illness. They helped her.

Kim and Candy had their own homes, so I can't speak about how they coped when they weren't with us, but it was obvious they were coming to terms in their unique ways. Whenever we got together, we shared our memories and tears. We still do. I also drew strength from work associates and friends who said little and listened much. They didn't pry, but weren't shy about asking, either. They gave me the openings I needed to talk about you. They never seemed to grow impatient as I lost my train of thought or repeated myself, or simply lapsed into silence. All our friends promised their prayers. The psalmist says of the Good Shepherd, "Thy rod and thy staff, they comfort me." So do good friends.

In those tortuous days, the biggest blow left me stunned, disoriented. Even though as a pastor I had seen the terrible stresses on a surviving family's relationships, I would never have guessed that our close family could be torn apart, even temporarily. Another example of my obtuseness. As my heart could not imagine one of us would ever commit suicide, neither could it believe that your death could separate any of us.

But the unthinkable happened.

My handling of your memorial services struck Candy as controlling and insensitive to the needs of the family. I sensed I was in trouble as we drove her to the airport for her return flight to California from the service in our church in Arizona, but I didn't know how much until her letter arrived. Anger she had bottled up for years blazed from the page. Accusations of my high-handedness going back to her youth came out. I was stunned. I had no idea she had harbored these feelings. She later asked me not to take her too seriously. She was not really herself when she wrote the letter, she explained. And I confessed I wasn't either; it seemed to take me forever to "get my mind back," to corral my flailing emotions. What made this period so difficult was, as I read and reread Candy's letter, I had to admit: guilty as charged.

I didn't know what to do. "The great Dr. Lawson," as Candy referred to me in her letter, didn't know what to do! My son whom I loved more than life itself was dead. In spite of your gracious letter, I had been tormenting myself with the "couldas" and "shouldas." Then came this proof that I had deeply wounded my daughter, and not just during our week together following your death but again and again throughout your teen and early adult years. I was devastated.

In that condition I had to walk to the pulpit each weekend and speak an "encouraging word from the Lord" to parishioners. I'm sure they sensed my grief but didn't suspect your death wasn't the only source.

A few years ago, a church member told me that in her college psychology class the professor asked students to name the person they believed had the most highly developed self-confidence, the healthiest ego-strength. She said she named me. I was taken aback at the time, because even then I couldn't see what she saw. In those days a pop-psychology term was making the rounds:

imposter syndrome. The term describes the paranoia of someone prominent in their field who harbors a fear of being found out, because they weren't what they seemed. That was me. I knew I wasn't up to the sometimes nearly overwhelming demands of my profession. I had fooled this trusting woman, that's all.

But I hadn't fooled my daughter. Whatever this parishioner might have perceived then, and whatever self-confidence I might have projected, had vanished now. I felt even more hesitant, unworthy. What did I have to tell these people? For fifteen years I had been their pastor. They had watched you kids grow up. They loved you. They accepted us as a normal family, with perhaps more than our share of stresses as we lived our demanding lives in full view of several thousand closely watching people. I had even asked the elders after about ten years whether they wanted to keep me on. I told them I was "damaged goods." It was evident you children were going to chart your own course and it wasn't the one your mother and I envisioned. The chairman reported the elders' decision between morning services in the hallway: "We decided you're not perfect," he said as he breezed by, "but don't quit."

I didn't. But my feelings of inadequacy then seemed like soaring self-confidence compared with what I was feeling in the aftermath of your death. Our son dead, a victim of his own hand. Our daughter distressed and scolding her father who, try as I might, couldn't convince myself she was wrong. Because she wasn't. How often I've thanked God since then that the breach separating Candy and me was temporary. We both reached out, hating the gulf between us, extending grace and forgiveness. We both determined we were not going to let this separation define our relationship going forward. We succeeded.

What, though, did I have left to give these people, I wondered? These faithful friends had been so patient with their pastor for so long? Did they think I was practicing what I preached—or did they now suspect I was a fraud, unable to draw strength from the Lord as I had always encouraged them to do? Had I been telling them the truth or just offering preacher talk?

Could I tell them the truth now? Could I admit I was hardly able to pray? Did I dare to let them know how deeply shaken my faith was? Not faith in God, although that took a beating, but faith in myself. I didn't blame God for your death, I couldn't blame God for our family's pain, and for certain I couldn't blame God for my all-too-evident shortcomings. Your mother and I accepted your insistence that this was your decision and yours alone. We respected you enough to believe you, even though the father in me persisted in asking maddening questions. I did remind God of the prayers your parents had raised all your life, pleading that God would protect you even from yourself. I couldn't help wondering why God didn't.

But my big loss of faith was in myself. When Candy wrote scathingly of "the great Dr. Lawson," I winced. If she only knew.

This isn't the end of the story, though. The family has urged me to quote from another letter Candy wrote me three years later. When your mother read it, she urged me to include it here, since it shows the forgiving, gracious side of Candy—and illustrates what it takes to hold a family together through a trauma like the one we endured in the months (years) after your death. Here it is. After some introductory words explaining what prompted her email, Candy writes:

> *Because of that and because I have been searching for some kind of understanding and peace about Lane, I began reading your letter to him* [the first feeble draft of this book]. *Got a whole 9 pages. Powerful stuff, Dad. Too, too powerful. Gonna be awhile before I am ready for the next 9. But I was left with an overwhelming need to explain something to you that I just realized I have known all along.*
>
> *In adulthood your children have found out what was hidden from us in childhood—a loving and wise father doesn't come pre-installed in every family unit. We never doubted your love, never. That's huge. So while I was reading your words of regret and self-reproach I felt a sense of urgency to communicate to you a realistic picture of your role in Lane's life, because it is apparent from your*

writing that you are pretty clueless (and I mean that with the greatest of respect).

The values you instilled in Lane are not what shortened his life, they are what lengthened it. If he hadn't been taught to serve, if you didn't push him to contribute, his motivation for living would have evaporated in high school. If you had done it any differently not only would his life have been shorter, he wouldn't have been much worth knowing. You gave him love and laughter, the two things that in my mind define who he was. And I don't mean simply that you loved him and you made him laugh. I mean you planted these things in his heart. He kept going for twenty-six years, until the body and mind were so weak that even his deep love for others and desire to serve just couldn't propel him any more. He hung on until he had given all that he felt he had. He hung on because of you. You gave him twenty-six years of life. You badgered him to make something of himself, kept him from wallowing in self-pity, turned his focus outward and would not let him quit. And every person whose life he touched owes you thanks. What you taught him was right on the mark. You taught him about Christ. And though he refused to talk the talk, he walked the walk, and all the joy he got out of life (which was considerable) he got from giving. I thank you from the bottom of my heart for giving to me the best friend I will ever have.

I don't have to tell you how grateful I am for Candy's kindness. She made possible the rapid healing of the wounds we felt within the family. Together we have weathered many storms, your death being by far the worst, but the truth is, we *have weathered* them—and every one of us contributed to our survival.

In addition to family stress, we all had to deal with the everyday tensions in other relationships. For me, of course, that meant performing on the job. In those first months after your death, preaching every weekend was a strenuous exercise in overcoming. I didn't want to do it. I wanted to hide. The people were gracious, as you would have expected. Several mentioned that my preaching had changed. Maybe. Probably. But what I noticed was how much more attentive they seemed to be. They appeared to hang onto every word, wondering, I suppose, whether I'd deal with the real issue on my heart or just hide behind the text. On this subject, at least, would I "come clean"? Just three weeks after returning to work, the sermon topic, assigned months earlier, was, "When Death Comes Anyway." Not easy.

In the beginning I seemed to be mentally resigning about three times a week. By the next spring, almost a year later, it had smoothed out to more like three times a month. My emotions were still unstable enough by late August after your May death that I decided to take the sabbatical leave I was eligible for next summer. It was a bad time to be away for four or five months, with the church in a building program and the college expanding in all directions, but I was afraid if I didn't have the sabbatical to look forward to (and to tie me down for the requisite year I owed the church and university afterward), I'd surrender to the nearly overpowering temptation to quit. Without it, I wondered whether I could keep going.

The whole experience of your departure ultimately strengthened my faith in God. As usual, your mother came through with equanimity, her quiet faith sustaining her, her strong identification with your illness giving her an empathy I couldn't muster. The struggle was really my own. What resulted couldn't be called a notable victory, but to be able to carry on at all was no mean achievement, at least to me. Having come this far in my spiritual odyssey, I didn't turn back, even though I wanted to.

So then, why didn't I quit? Here's why. Even though my self-confidence was shattered, I still felt called. Over the years I had fantasized about other careers I could pursue. Surely they weren't as demanding, wouldn't subject me to so much criticism, wouldn't require so much of my family. The day you were born, for example, I was pretty certain I'd have to change professions. Your delivery was difficult. When you finally emerged from the birth canal you looked so battered the nurses wouldn't show you to your mother until they absolutely had to. They were afraid you would scare her. You scared me. I was afraid you might have suffered brain damage and I would need to quit teaching and get a job that would pay better so we'd have the money for your care. Thankfully, within a day your swelling receded, the doctors reassured, and I didn't have to leave my rewarding but low-paying profession.

There were other times as well, but in the darkness following your death, when returning to the job seemed such a daunting challenge that I wondered how I could do it, this time I couldn't picture myself doing anything else. I couldn't conceive of more important, more fulfilling work. So I didn't resign. It helped that no one urged me to leave. The college offered the same encouraging support as the church. Colleagues on both campuses kept up their prayer vigils and whenever possible eased the workload. I felt carried by their support and affection. What a debt I owe them!

And though perplexed by God's standing by and letting you go ahead with your terrible plan, I couldn't turn my back on God, either. At the end of the day, when I had poured out my grief, I realized I was praying as if God was really there. In spite of everything, I believed. And, disabled though I was, I ultimately desired nothing more than to keep serving, relying more on God's strength than my own.

There was another reason. I couldn't prevent your death, even though I've been able to help prevent others ("He saved others; why couldn't he save his son?"). What I was unable to do for you, I wanted—still want—to do for others, if they'll have me. Nothing else matters as much now.

4

What I Don't Regret

"WE HAD NO UNFINISHED business," I said in my remarks at your memorial service. No arguments unresolved, no lingering animosity, no deep regrets of a ruptured relationship. A few months after your death, a couple in Oregon asked to meet with me. Their twenty-something son had also taken his life. Their grief was almost unbearable, for them and so, as I was still barely managing my own, for me. There was a huge difference, though. When he died, he and his parents were estranged. He had long abused alcohol and drugs; he was into Satanism. With acrimony he had flung his final words at them. Their wounds were deep. So much unfinished business.

You spared us.

Of course, I have gone over the "I wish I had" list many, many times. But that list is balanced by another equally long and infinitely more satisfying one, the "I'm glad we did . . ." list. Here are some of the items:

Vacations

Overseas trips

Interruptions in my study

Bathroom talks

"Open house"

Our dates

The old blue sofa
The laughter.

Vacations

I'm frequently accused of workaholism. "Not guilty," I retort and offer as one proof of my innocence our record of vacations. As far as your memory would reach you could recount tales of our infamous camping expeditions, our impromptu getaways, our transcontinental journeys. The most famous was the one with Grandpa and Grandma Whitney. We all headed out from Tennessee bound for visiting relatives in Oregon, our station wagon and their pickup truck stuffed to overflowing, a family straight out of television's "Beverly Hillbillies." We camped one night near Wyoming's Flaming Gorge. Even before we'd finished setting up camp you promptly set out to explore the territory. Before long you bounded back with a grin to proudly showed us your discovery: a handful of "bullets." We had a little difficulty convincing you they were deer droppings. Your sisters were not impressed with your findings. "Bullets" has remained in the family vocabulary ever since.

Oregon was often our destination, an ambitious one in the days when our vacation was two or three weeks. It took us at least four days to drive from Johnson City, Tennessee, and three from Indianapolis to get to our extended families on the West Coast. Later on, the trek northward from Arizona was less demanding, a mere twenty-four hours. You three were driver-licensed teenagers then, urging me to let us drive straight through so we wouldn't burn up precious vacation hours just getting there. "We can take turns driving, Dad," was your promise, one unfailingly forgotten as you slept through the night—so the twelve-to-five shift inevitably fell to me. You woke up one by one, each apologizing profusely. You hadn't meant to abandon me, you said. You had sincerely meant to take your turn, you said. I yawned.

What do I remember of those annual vacations? Many miles on the road, much singing—especially the Lawson family song ("Oh we ain't got a barrel of money / Maybe we're ragged and funny / But we're travelin' along, / Singing a song, / Side by side")—nearly continuous laughter, an occasional stop alongside the road to separate the squabbling siblings, more laughter, and the boundless curiosity of three bright children who didn't want to miss anything. (Well, that may be stretching it! There were also those exasperating times when you missed the magnificent scenery, too busy with whatever held your attention in the back seat. A generational difference, I'm afraid.) Fortunately, as you grew older, "Are we almost there yet?" disappeared.

We often took our vacation trips in conjunction with our church's annual national convention somewhere in America. When you children were still quite young, you were already seasoned travelers, the envy of your schoolmates. You made friends wherever we went—including with the Staton children in Missouri, where you, Lane, first became intimately acquainted with poison oak.

We didn't have much money in those days. Preachers and Christian college professors don't earn high salaries, but we saved around the calendar for our summer vacations and accumulated enough in the kitty for some great excursions.

Lane and Grandpa Whitney show off their big catch

Overseas trips

You were a world traveler by the time you graduated from high school. Your year as an exchange student in Germany was a little hard on us—how we missed you!—but it fit right into the life-style we had adopted years earlier. A minister enjoys so many benefits; for us that included some international conventions. A favorite was the one in Mexico City in 1974, where you mastered the art of piñata demolition. Another perk was leading tour groups to the Holy Land. You had been to the Middle East twice before even entering high school. You could rattle off the names of countries you had visited: Israel, Egypt, Jordan, Switzerland, Austria, Turkey, Greece, Mexico.

When I reflect on those tours, I picture you as an elementary-school-aged boy valiantly wrestling the older ladies' overstuffed suitcases off the airport carousel or out of the tour buses and into the hotels, or posing atop ruined columns in Ephesus, or bobbing in the Dead Sea, or sitting astride a camel in Jordan, or. . . .

No regrets here.

Interruptions in my study

Another blessing of the ministry: I could do much of my work at home. In Tennessee, Indiana, and Arizona I kept a study in which to read, prepare classes, and write sermons. You were respectful of my workplace.

You were also welcome. When you appeared at the door to announce your need to talk, I'd quickly finish what I was doing, or find a place to pause, and the conversation would commence. Sometimes it was about nothing in particular. Other times about your important issues. I don't remember much about the content. What lingers with me is how glad I was—and am—that we could talk.

No unfinished business.

Bathroom talks

These magical, impromptu moments were even better than the study conversations. They were Arizona phenomena, mostly, when you three were adolescents, although I recall similar happy meetings in Indiana. How did they begin? Your mother and I might be brushing our teeth or I might be shaving when one of you kids would come in to ask something, and then something else. Another would overhear and join the conversation, and then the other. Before long all five of us (even more, when Brian and Rosa lived with us) would be there, sitting on the counter or the floor, laughing and chatting about something—or nothing—but no one leaving, no one wanting to break the spell. To this day, when such serendipity occurs, wherever it happens, we call it a "bathroom" conversation. I can't help wondering what that must conjure up in the mind of the uninitiated eavesdropper.

"Open house"

My parents' home was a fairly closed affair. My timid mother was never comfortable entertaining company. Things had to be perfect before you could open your home. They were seldom perfect; therefore, we didn't have many guests. I suspect this was an outgrowth of the increasing tension between my parents, because in the earlier years of their marriage they did on occasion host a Sunday School class or other church group. Dad loved to have people in. But with their growing alienation, hosting virtually stopped.

How much I have appreciated your mother's gift of hospitality. I could invite friends or new acquaintances in without warning. She would whip up a good meal from the stock at hand—which was often precious little toward the end of the month. I was so proud of her I overdid it, but she never complained. She still doesn't.

You children took after me. It was the most natural thing in the world to bring your playmates home when you were small children, and you were still making your home their home in your high school years. When you left, we not only missed you, but we missed your friends as well.

One special Saturday evening stands out. Candy and Mom were out of town on a school outing of some sort, you were staying overnight with a friend (was it John?), and Kim and I were going to have the house to ourselves. I was looking forward to the evening, since she and I had so little time together and all too soon she'd be graduating from high school and moving on to college. We'd have a chance to enjoy each other's company, a special father-daughter moment.

It was not to be. Early in the evening the phone rang and then the doorbell. The quiet evening for two erupted into a rowdy evening for seven: Kim and her dad and Brian and Mark P. and Mark R. and Kevin and Bruce.

That's pretty much how it was for years.

No regrets.

Our dates

By the time you three were in your teens, we didn't date as much as we used to. You developed other interests and had pretty full schedules. But in your younger years we dated regularly. Mom didn't work outside the home in those days, so she could spend quality time with each of you. My workload was always heavy; to compensate we adopted Dad's Dating Policy. Once a week I'd take one of you out to dinner. You picked the restaurant, set the agenda, and selected the menu. May I now confess how much I disliked Big Macs? Still do. But Big Macs were your meal of choice as children. It was your night, so Big Macs it was! (When you were teenagers, I secretly wished for a return to those cheaper MacDonald's days. By then you had more discriminating palates. How my wallet hated those tempting full-color menus, luring you from away from cheap hamburgers to more costly fare.) These were dates, I tried to remember; they were not to be hijacked as venues for another of Dad's sermons. My role was to listen, not to lecture. Whatever was on your minds became the program for the evening.

What was on the program? Not much, most of the time. Sometimes we just ate quietly together, savoring the French fries. (McDonald's does do French fries right!) The date nights paid off later, when you really did have things on your mind you wanted to talk about. We had already learned how to talk to one another—and how to listen.

I didn't much like, but I sure don't regret, the Big Macs.

The old blue sofa

You inherited it. It was only right that you should, since you were the last to leave home and by then the old faithful servant had done its job. Mom bought it from Penney's in Nashville when you were just three. It served the family until it could barely hold us up. Mom earned the money during my doctoral studies, when we managed 120 married-student apartments for Vanderbilt University. She scrubbed eighty-five ovens that year as she prepped the flats for new tenants. With the pocket money she made, the only extra money we had in those frugal days, she bought the sofa for our home back in Johnson City. Then we transferred it with us to Indiana and on to Arizona. When you set up housekeeping on your own in Phoenix, the sofa went with you. Only when you moved to Oregon, and with some sadness, did you retire it.

In the beginning the sofa was an attractive piece of furniture, velvety aqua-marine fabric (which was "in" in those days) with soft cushions, long enough to hold us all, as it frequently did, along with an assortment of your friends who happened to be around. Always a "huggy-touchy" family, we all tended to bypass other sitting options on our way to the sofa, where we could literally be in touch with each other.

Every family needs an old blue sofa.

The laughter

We produced our share of shouts and tears as well, but what lingers is the reverberation of the laughter. We were usually a quiet bunch. We granted one another plenty of space for reading, handcrafts, puzzles, chores, homework, practicing, or whatever. But when we came together, we laughed.

And you were frequently the cause of it. Even when you weren't feeling good, you liked to tease. A favorite among our pictures is one taken the last Christmas you spent with us, with a package ribbon wrapped around your head like a sweatband. You looked ridiculous.

Lane's last Christmas with us. The gift he's opening was for his upcoming January Desert Survival School adventure.

You *were* ridiculous, a man's body camouflaging a boy's impishness. Until we retired them, the dining room chairs bore the scars of that same Christmas, when you gave your little nephews some stringy putty—designed for outdoors—and then demonstrated its indoor virtues, where it left its indelible marks. I could tell I was mellowing in my old age, because you got away with it.

You and your sisters often made me the butt of your laughter, especially as our friendship grew in your adolescent years. Even when you were young, though, you weren't afraid to laugh at me. Two moments leap to mind. The first is when I paraded my brand new doctoral robe before the family. It cost me a lot to buy that academic gown, and I was showing off. Kim, speaking for all three of you children, announced, "Daddy, you look ridiculous in that dress." I suppose I did.

The other one caught me by surprise as I entered the family room. My three by-now-teenaged children had somehow got ahold of my high school yearbook. (Yearbooks should be locked up until one's children have themselves become ridiculous adults!) You'd seen enough to come to your conclusion, which you gleefully announced: "Dad, you really were a nerd, weren't you?"

Yes, I really was. Might as well laugh about it.

So we did.

No regrets here.

5

What I Do Regret

I REGRET WORKING TOO much. If we could live these years over, I like to think I'd be different. Yet I wonder. My father spent less time with his three than I did with you three. I always felt like a slacker compared to him. He was twenty-nine years older than I, yet most of his life I had trouble keeping up with him. The man could work!

I haven't been consciously trying to compete with him. Subconsciously? Who knows? It feels more physical than psychological, like I wasn't built to sit down, like something in the genes is overheating. I need to keep moving to burn off the excess energy.

Yet I also have to admit the insecurities, the need to prove something, that drove me through the doctoral program. I've been running scared most of my life, in one way or another, with a church to serve, a career to build, a reputation to establish, a family to nurture, a university to lead, and of course, bills to pay. I'm sure I haven't identified all my demons. Identified or not, they did succeed in pushing me too often to the brink of exhaustion. And the family paid.

It's often been pointed out that at a funeral nobody ever pauses over the corpse to praise the deceased for putting in all that overtime at the office. What matters is the relationships, not the extra pay. The irony in the ministry is that you don't get paid for overtime. You just put it in.

My long hours didn't seem to hurt you. Your social calendar, even when you were young, was full. So I don't think I damaged you, but I wish we had spent more time together for my sake, if not for yours. You know that old song? "You never get enough of that wonderful stuff." Time with you was wonderful stuff.

I have one other regret. My failure to assist you to return to your Christian walk. Those were proud moments when, one by one, I had the privilege (this isn't a cliché—it *was* a privilege) of baptizing each of you children. I choked up each time, predictably. You were sincere. You were ready.

Then came the teen years when your religious struggle began. As I said earlier, we didn't panic, Mom and I, because we could remember. That wasn't precisely stated, I guess. Your mother didn't go through a religious rebellion as a teenager, even though her father was a minister. She's another one I don't fully understand. She says she's always been "a pleaser." That may explain why she didn't give her parents any worries as an adolescent, and why she never (outwardly, at least) rebelled against their teachings.

I didn't either, outwardly, but my irritatingly skeptical mind challenged the "givens" and forced an examination of every church tenet. Religious struggles bedeviled me more in my twenties than in my teens; many questions weren't resolved until I was well into my thirties. And frankly, some of them still aren't.

Your decision to plot your own course didn't surprise or offend us. My regret is that time ran out before you had completed your investigation, and that I wasn't of more help along the way. Obviously, I'm a convinced follower of Christ or I couldn't do what I do. However, I share your criticism of many of Christianity's trappings and have often confessed that I am not, as the term is usually defined, a religious man. But at the core of the Christian faith stands Jesus, "the way, the truth, and the life." I stand with him.

As I said, I regret I couldn't convince you when we still had time.

When a good friend of mine read this part of the manuscript, she took me to task. She didn't think I was being fair. "Lane's faith was Lane's faith." In other words, Dad, get off his case! She's right. This section is too much about me! But, then, I'm afraid this whole book is about me, about my struggle to learn to accept the unacceptable. I really do sound self-indulgent. I'm sorry. I agree with what my friendly critic adds, "You can tell he was an inherently spiritual soul. In my experience, many who take their own lives are. They see the pain of life a little too clearly. His final note is full of spirituality—'curious about what comes next'—'on to better things'—and finally, 'I love you.'"

So far so good. I'm grateful for this encouragement. But then she hits me between the eyes: "I suppose this is a hard question, and who am I to ask it, but who needed him to come back to a more traditional form of Christian faith? You? Joy? Your readers?" So I have to ask myself, what is this about, anyway, this unseemly longing for you to come closer, ever closer, to the faith of *your* father? It's a flaw I share with many, I'm afraid, measuring the orthodoxy of others by the standard of our own personal beliefs and practices. *I do it, so it must be right. I believe it, so it must be true.* This whole conversation with you has done so much to make me face up to my own egocentricity, just as Candy's letter did. I too much enjoy being the center of a universe, my universe. It was my self-absorption that kept me from clearly hearing Candy's anguish before she had to write it in her letter; I was too wrapped up in my own hurt. And here my friend catches me fretting unduly over your spiritual odyssey, fretting more for my sake than yours, she thinks.

She goes on: "You did not fail because you did not bring him back to traditional Christian faith. You and Joy succeeded in giving him the ego strength to leave it in the first place and begin his age-appropriate questioning journey. We both know he likely would have made his way back on his own, without any help from family. You don't choose a romantic interest who is staunchly Christian if you aren't already on the way back."

She's right. You didn't need our help. What did I just tell you? Fathers are fixers. So are pastors. Some things just need to be left up to others.

6

What Has Changed

THE OTHER DAY MOM and I were talking again about the contrast between your healthy appearance and your sickly body. A person can't tell what inner battles someone is fighting by looking on the outside. "I've had to give up judging," I told her. "Me, too," she agreed.

A simple enough statement, but an enormous confession for this pastor. Your Aunt Betty more than once reminded me what an intense young preacher I was, full of conviction and, she charged, judgment. Woe to those persons whose opinions differed from yours! Her memory sometimes clashes with her younger brother's, yet here she might be close to the truth. Once convinced, I do tend to be a little stubborn.

"Tended" might be the better word. I'm feeling more agreeable these days. Having so badly misjudged your condition, I wonder whether I'll ever again be able to read others as I once thought I could. If that "ability" is gone, it's a good loss.

For that matter, I'm less certain of myself in general. More "perhapses" and "maybes" now. Old doubts, long ago wrestled to the ground, have sprung up for another round. Prayer, for example. Yes, we've "felt" the support of our praying friends, as I mentioned. And I sometimes pray, although perfunctorily at times, more from duty than pleasure, often with greater uncertainty than awe. Arguments against prayer—it's an appeal to magic, it's a delusion of the weak, it's absurd to ask God to rearrange the universe to satisfy your personal whim, it's an immature person's comforting ritual—these won't leave me alone, especially when I recall the many prayers for you. Yet I can't help praying; I actually do have more confidence in God's strength than my own. Fortunately, when my efforts are feeble, others faithfully pray for me. I shamelessly rely on them to carry me through.

One lifelong doubt: do I belong in the ministry? This one drove me from preaching when I was twenty-seven. I could only return to the pastorate eight years later when I finally caught on that I didn't have to *be* the example to the flock but to *point to* the example, Christ. People expect their pastor to be holy. That terrifies me, now more than ever. And when I read the lives of the saints, or even hang around some of my saintly friends (I have several), I wonder how I dare presume. I tell others about a Lord who can make us new, with whose help we can overcome obstacles—this coming from a man who still has so much growing up to do.

You and I have talked enough about these doubts before. I bring them up again thinking you might be interested to know that in some ways I'm right back where you were, starting over, learning to trust again, wishing I were otherwise.

One change has been for the better. Having confessed I couldn't fully understand what you were suffering, I can add that through you I've grown more sympathetic. Tears have always come easily, as you know, but I've never had to fight them back as I do now. I embarrass myself. In sermons I've often referred to the church as a community of suffering. This is theologically accurate. Now, though, it is more *our* community of suffering. I'm somewhat like Father Damien, who in the beginning addressed the members of his leper colony in Hawaii, "You lepers," but after contracting the disease himself, he ended his days of preaching, "*We* lepers. . . ." The tears are, I repeat, embarrassing, but my identifying with suffering soulmates is for real.

I'm hesitant to tell you what else has happened, because it would be easy for you to misunderstand. I hope I've convinced you that, if I had a choice in the matter, I wouldn't have given you up for anything. But neither would I want to go back to being the person I was before you died. How can I explain? A new depth has entered, a new seriousness, a sense of being more in touch with reality. Aeschylus said, "Wisdom comes through suffering." Yes, but I can't claim that wisdom is what your loss has given me.

Instead, it's more like a broadened perspective. This incident will explain it. At our family vacation at Cultus Lake the summer after you left us, your new brother-in-law David buried Jeff's Jeep in the lake. What a way to introduce yourself to your new in-laws, don't you think? Jeff and David had just launched Brian's Wave Runner (a two-seated jet ski). As Jeff was taking off for a test run around the lake, David volunteered to drive the Jeep and trailer from the ramp to the parking lot. He dropped it into gear, released the clutch, and promptly backed into the water. He stopped, decided the ramp must be steeper than he thought, pushed the accelerator harder, released the clutch—and went faster and deeper into the lake. Jeff's daughter Kristin, watching from the shore and aware of the sudden drop-off at the bottom of the ramp, yelled, "Get out of the Jeep." He did, barely in time. As Jeff returned on the Wave Runner, he wondered where his Jeep was. He didn't see it up in the parking lot. It wasn't on the ramp. Then, coming closer, he spotted the vehicle— that is, the inch or two of it still above water.

Jeff prepares to unbury his Jeep

You can imagine how David felt. You don't have to guess. Picture him sitting on the ramp in a vertical fetal position, arms hugging his knees, rocking. His first words to Jeff were, "I owe you a Jeep." Fortunately, Jeff's a mechanical whiz. He pulled his truck onto the ramp, attached a cable to Jeep and truck, dove down to shift the Jeep into neutral, returned to the truck and pulled the drowned vehicle out of the water. Then he set to work restoring it. It took him a mere three hours. For a while David could hardly talk except to apologize. The rest of us were thanking God it was David and not ourselves; we could have made the same mistake. The Jeep looked new, but it wasn't. The reverse position of its old-fashioned three-speed gearshift is to the left and up—where first gear is located in most four-speed vehicles. There was no diagram on the gearshift knob so David, who had never driven a three-speed, couldn't have known. What he thought was first gear forward was instead reverse. (When I tell the story I always add, "It wasn't his fault. He was too young. Only thirty." All of us old-timers learned to drive cars with standard three-speed transmissions; David's age group learned on four-speeds—or automatic transmissions. See, sometimes it's a good thing to be older.)

We sympathized with David and celebrated his near-miss. Of course, he later had to take a lot of good-natured ribbing. I knew he'd recovered by Friday when, as I lazed in the kayak, David tried to drown me in the jet ski's wake. In those tense first moments, though, when David was so embarrassed he couldn't look at us, Brian made the speech I wanted to make, but I couldn't get the words out. My emotions muted me. He told David, "This is just a Jeep. When you've lost as much as these men have lost, what's a Jeep?" It had been just five years since Jeff and Joan's son Shawn was killed on his dad's motorcycle, and just one year since you died. Compared with the loss of a son, what's the loss of a Jeep?

There was a day when I would have taken the Jeep incident much more seriously. You know. You could tell stories that make me blush now, of the times when you must have wondered about my priorities, when I became upset about this or that *something*. They were skewed, no doubt. What can compare in value to a son or a daughter? What *thing* can upset me as much as it once did, what loss equal to the loss of a child?

Silence has become more precious, too. "Be still and know that I am God" makes more sense now than ever. Our world is plagued with too much talking, too many words often hurled in anger; they confuse, abuse, maim. You came to that conclusion before I did. You often sought the silence of the forest. Yet you learned, you told us, that you were too much a people person to be alone indefinitely. Me, too. But I cherish solitude now and have become increasingly impatient with the too much talking of my profession.

I'm not doing a very good job of describing the difference between the before and the after, I'm afraid. What have I gained that I wouldn't give up? The only way I can express it is that I seem to think more deeply, feel more intensely, and identify with others more completely than before I lost you. And I give thanks more quickly, and for more, even for little favors once taken for granted. If you'll allow me—and not think this is just more preacher talk—God seems closer. Do you find it strange that you who weren't so certain about God should be the instrument through whom I have drawn nearer to God?

Funerals (we call them "celebrations of life" now, but they're the same thing) have become extremely difficult, though. It takes all the self-control I can muster not to make a fool of myself. Shortly after you died, I was asked to conduct a memorial service for a twenty-something woman who died of cancer. I didn't want to do it, didn't feel up to it. I reluctantly agreed to, though, provided the mother would forgive me if I choked up. She was gracious and I got through it, but the pain I felt for the grieving parents—and this still grieving one—threatened both tears and muteness.

It isn't just parents I cry for. Every loss, no matter what the age of the deceased, is wrenching, and every mourning survivor a brother or sister or other loved one in distress. What makes matters worse is that this pastor, whose tools are words, often can't find the right ones for comforting.

We experienced the inadequacy of words when people tried to comfort us. They couldn't find the right ones, either. I suppose there aren't any, not really. Those well-meaning souls who thought they knew just what to say may have satisfied themselves, but they left us cold. Each misguided attempt hurt doubly. I hurt for them, that they so misunderstood. And I hurt for myself, because their clumsiness reminded me of my own and made me recall how many times I must have offended or surprised others by my mumbled condolences, the ready verse of scripture, and what must have seemed a perfunctory prayer. Yet I wonder whether I'm any more helpful now, when I simply want to hug or hold a hand or cry.

Karen McKowen's sympathy card is the one we've quoted more than any other. I have no idea what the printed lines said. What Mom and I remember so vividly are the words Karen scratched in the bottom margin: "It isn't fair." She caught our mood exactly. It wasn't, it isn't, it will never seem to be fair that you were taken. That's what we felt. Karen gave us permission to admit it.

We learned long ago that life *isn't* fair. The way to madness is to demand justice for ourselves. But equally maddening are the theological platitudes so glibly proffered: God wanted Lane to be with him, God had a plan and Lane's suicide was part of it, or (incredibly, as if you could take this seriously) you must never question the sovereign will of God. How can you *not* question it? And how can you think that repeating some religious cliché will heal an aching heart?

Too many words.

One final change. The gospel has taken on deepened significance. "For God so loved the world that he gave his only son. . . ." I've quoted these words all my life and thought I appreciated them. That was before I gave my son. Not that I did give you, of course. I wouldn't have, not willingly. That's the distance between God's universal and my particular love, I suppose. I didn't voluntarily give, but I *had to* give up my son. I had no choice. God did. But God has powers I lack; God could give Jesus, knowing God could get him back. Would he have allowed the cross and tomb without a resurrection and ascension? That would be asking too much, even of God.

There's the promise of heaven, of course, and reunion there. That's comforting. But that's then and this is now, and in the present I am powerless. I can't call you back. You're gone; in my moody moments I remember those long workdays and crowded schedules and hours stolen from the family, and I bitterly accuse myself, "For Roy so loved the ministry that he gave his only son. . . ." A nearly blasphemous thought, and I regret but can't totally erase it.

The Bible says God gave his son willingly.

What kind of love is this? To care so much, to bear so much. Even with God's power, the agony of Jesus' death had to have been magnified in the Father's heart.

Such is the cost of salvation.

As you can see, I identify with God, giving his son for the sake of the world. Incredible love, beyond my imitating, but I identify, anyway. On the other hand, I take my place as the believer saved through the death of the son. I was first saved through the death of God's son.

My second transformation has to be credited to my son, for I was in a sense reborn through your death. The old man is dead, and I never want to see him again. The new man is who he is because of your sacrifice. And just as I give thanks in all things for the grace of God through Jesus, I now am conscious of my debt to you. I doubt I'll ever be able to give thanks for your death, but I am regularly giving thanks for what your sacrifice has done for me and who I am becoming because of it.

Does this make sense?

Let me give you an example. After I preached the assigned sermon on the subject of steadfastness at the closing session of the North American Christian Convention in 1995, the year after you died, several people offered their compliments. I had to fight the temptation to snap back, "Do you have any idea what that sermon cost me?" In it I talked about you. I confessed how hard it was to carry on after you left. Please forgive me, but I was identifying with God in the loss of his son. Yet inwardly I confessed, "I paid too high a price."

The mysterious effect continues, though. From England comes a letter from a young man who says he had learned of your death—and it saved his life. He was despondent, he writes, and was at the brink of suicide when he heard from one of our English friends about you. Our friend told him of our devastation. The young man realized he couldn't go through with his plan; he would hurt too many too deeply. In our trip to England a year later he sought me out and we talked further about his struggles.

Your death saved his life.

His is not the only one. Letters have come from other persons who heard your story. They have thanked me for talking about you. They have been encouraged to carry on, they said.

You saved their lives, too. You have become to them, in ways you could never have foreseen, the messenger of good news. Death can bring deliverance. The awful day of Jesus' death is not inappropriately named, after all: it is *Good* Friday, for from his death comes life.

You would feel very uncomfortable with this pairing of your death with Jesus'; I'm not at ease exploring the theme, either, but it's an example of the type of rethinking of the gospel and its consequences that you have forced on me. Just as Jesus' birth requires us to view every birth as more than the result of the union of sperm and egg, so the consequences of his crucifixion compel us to look for the good in every death. Yours, Son, has already saved and transformed many lives, beginning with mine.

As we sang "Spirit of the Living God / Fall afresh on me,"
Mom pointed out this "crown of thorns."

7

More Than Blood Family

SOME READING THESE PAGES will undoubtedly be a little confused by the references to "adopted" or "Velcro" children. You,
Lane, helped us build the Velcro family along with Kim and
Candy. We've never gone to court to legally add to our family, but
over the years we've invited several to join us. Some have never
left. Like Velcro, they stick.

We began early, your mother and I, with Carole, a Tigard
(Oregon) High School student during my teaching days there.
She was at odds with her family and needed some space until they
could be reconciled thirteen months later.

When we were at Vanderbilt in Nashville, an unmarried girl
from our Tigard (Oregon) church lived with us until her baby was
born. We arranged for his adoption and cared for her until she was
ready to be on her own. In those days a pregnant teenager bore
a stigma in polite society. When her parents asked us to take her
in we gladly did. Our church also openly accepted her. We were
proud she was part of our family.

While in Indiana, we hosted a young man just out of prison
along with his four-year-old daughter. I'm afraid we weren't able
to help him any. We hated to say goodbye to the little girl when
we finally had to invite her con artist father to leave. We weren't
yet "Velcroing."

Subsequent experiments in expanded family living were
happier. Some stayed with us for a while, but not long enough

to forge permanent bonds. Others are still with us, like Carolyn in Indiana, the elementary school teacher who became a second mother to you. She nicknamed you Poo Bear. You hated the name but loved her.

We hadn't been in Arizona long before Brian became your Velcro brother. He dated Kim a couple of times but when their dating was over he didn't go away. Then we were joined Kim's friend Rosa, an Ecuadoran exchange student. With Brian and Rosa, we now had—for a short time—five teenagers in the house. The girls each had a bedroom. Brian got the family room couch and you, Lane, always the accommodating one, slept on the floor behind the couch. Those were happy days.

Thus it began. The family kept growing. (Actually, it still does. At our most recent annual all-family vacation, more than fifty of us were together in Branson, including several branches: Terrill, Ronde, Phillips, Reynolds, Thompson, Ohanessian, Widmer. And this list doesn't include the others who were unable to attend.)

I skipped the first of these adopted kids, Jeff Terrill. It startles people when I introduce him as our "oldest Velcro son," because Jeff's only eight years younger than I am and at six-foot-four-inches towers above me. But when he was a sixteen-year-old and I was his twenty-four-year-old pastor, he thought me old enough to be his father. And so I became. Although he never lived in our home, he's lived in our hearts from the beginning. He and Joan gave our Kim's name to their firstborn. Now we claim several generations of Terrills as our own.

I hope you'll understand when I tell you how glad we are that we never limited our family just to our blood kin. Thanks to Velcroing, we not only have our two cherished daughters and their husbands and their offspring but also other daughters and sons and their offspring who have been welcomed into our family. In your Mom's and my hour of greatest need, this big, wonderful Velcro family joined Kim and Candy in propping us up. Brian, for example, never left our side from the moment he learned of your death until we all returned to Arizona after your services in Oregon.

The same was true of Jeff. I hated to make the phone call to give him our sad news. Lifting the receiver, I remembered the day five years earlier when Jeff had telephoned us with the stunning word that Shawn, their twenty-one-year-old son, had been killed.

How could I gently break the news of your death to this man who had been my son since he was a teenager? Somehow the words came out. And as we knew they would, the Terrills immediately broke camp and headed home. Until we returned from Oregon nearly two weeks later, Jeff and Joan never left our side, either. Thanks to their motorhome, all of us (including Kim and her husband, Candy, Brian, and Grandma and Grandpa Whitney) could travel together to Brookings from Portland with Jeff and Joan.

Those days together in the motorhome as we waited for clearance so we could have your memorial service made us aware as never before that we were in fact one family, not held together by blood but by love. We didn't know it then, but that week would be repeated each year in our all-family vacation, bringing us together from Oregon, Washington, California, Arizona, Indiana, Missouri, and as far away as Australia.

We didn't even wait another year. The first Christmas after you left us the whole family (except for our Indianapolis Hollingsworths) came to our home in Arizona. It was the first time the Terrills had celebrated the holiday with us but, remembering their first Christmas without Shawn, they knew how much we would need them. It was also a first for Jeff, whose natural parents were dead. Since Jeff and Joan's marriage every Christmas had naturally been celebrated with Joan's family. This year, he remarked, "Now I have a family." And the Velcro family has continued to grow, with the Jacobs and the Reynolds and the Phillipses and the Domkes and the Painchauds and Faye and Lorraine and Loretta and Alice and. . . .

No one can ever take your place, Lane, but you'll get it when I tell you that, since we can't have you, we're more grateful than ever that we have never closed the circle of our family.

Here I go, sounding like a preacher again, but I can't help thinking of a slogan Christians love to repeat: "You can't outgive

God." It's the short version of Ecclesiastes 11:1, "Cast thy bread upon the waters: for thou shalt find it after many days." When I first began trying to connect with Jeff, I had no idea that one day I would be leaning on him. And when Brian started hanging around the house, we could not have predicted that he'd become Uncle Brian to a passel of Lawson grandchildren, taking over the pleasurable duties you used to tackle with such panache.

What's true of our Velcro family is also true of our friends. I started to mention a few names and quit, fearing I'd leave out too many. We were astonished at how many came to what we thought would be our private family service for you. They drove and flew in from Seattle to the north and Los Angeles area to the south. They called us from as far away as Japan, asking directions to Brookings. We were overwhelmed by their outpouring of love. Then came the cards and letters. Never has a family been more blessed in friendships than ours.

8

Our Return to the Rock

MOM AND I HAD planned to return to The Rock during the Oregon section of our sabbatical leave the next year after our communion service for you. We both assumed—without talking about it—that this pilgrimage would be an essential ingredient of any future trip to our home state. We had been looking forward to it. The day before, though, I began mentally resisting. I didn't want to go back. When I admitted how I was feeling, I don't think she understood. She had already returned once; she was eager to go again. For me, I guess it was too soon after speaking at the North American Christian Convention, when my emotions were laid bare again, this time before thousands of people. Whatever the reason, I was withdrawing, sinking deeper into silence. Words weren't working for me.

We returned anyway.

We hardly spoke as we parked the car and wended our way down the steep slippery path to the sandy beach, gingerly stepping on exposed rocks across the little creek. Then we stood, arms entwined, on the spot where, nearly fourteen months earlier, we took the bread and the wine—and surrendered your ashes to the wind and the waves. The breeze blew even harder than it had a year ago. We had to brace ourselves against it. The tide was out; starfish and sea anemones were basking in the sun. Mom said once again she was glad you weren't hurting now. I mumbled some response. I had shut down. I wanted only quiet, oblivion.

Is this the essence of acceptance? No questions, few tears, my soul at peace, able to push back against the forceful wind, but without irritation; then, sitting on the rock, arms sheltering your mother from the insistent gusts, absorbing her warmth, saying nothing, wanting nothing, eyes resting on the turbulent surf. Not even praying. Words seemed inappropriate, intrusive. I wanted just *to be*. Nothing more.

View from The Rock, a year later

We made our way down from the rock's ledge to the long path leading to the car. We paused a moment on the sand and I saw you again, the ruggedly handsome youth whose blond features made me suspect a Scandinavian ancestor somewhere in the gene stock. There you were, grasping your grandfather's fishing pole at the water's edge, hoping for a record catch. Or at least one fish. Then my mind flashed further back to the little towhead digging in the sand, splashing in the tidepools, absorbed in wonder and joy.

Lane "splashing."

Your Pacific Paradise. And then I smiled at the young adult leaning against his Volkswagen "Thing," proud owner of the yellow
Jeep-like vehicle that never quite lived up to its promise but did
teach you much about what makes an automobile run. The domi-
nant, abiding image: the smiling face. I asked—yet again—how

was it possible that such a wholesome, thoroughly charming human being could take his life?

Lane with his "Thing." That's The Rock in the background.

We had to keep moving. My mind once more went blank. We crossed the creek and trudged back up the hill toward our return to reality.

That's when I almost disappointed Mom again. She asked to veer off to the left, to wade through the waist-deep grass to our old cabin. She wanted one more look at the place where you had camped that first year of your Oregon experiment. I had seen enough, reminisced enough. But her desire trumped my reluctance. I followed her lead. The cabin had always been special to all of us. Your grandfather built it nearly forty years earlier, a tiny ten-by-twelve-foot two-story shelter (although "two-story" is misleading; a shelf overhead could accommodate two sleeping bags, little else). The primitive structure (comparable to today's popular tiny houses, but without plumbing or electricity) now sagged under the weight of years and neglect, derelict, abandoned, depressing. The porch had all but disappeared, the surviving weather-ravaged boards rotten, not to be trusted. The windows nothing but scattered shards jutting out from decaying casings. The leaking, useless roof. Mr. Whitney had created his cabin with care; the current owners, if they hadn't forgotten about it, couldn't have cared less. We quickly surveyed the remains, then set out once more through the tall grass toward the car.

Our route led through the meadow; once again we paused. It was in this meadow, on the day of your private memorial service, that we came together, first one, then another, then yet another until we were all standing there, mutely gazing at The Rock, lost in our individual reflections. Someone began to sing. Before long the rest joined in. It was spontaneous—praise songs and choruses and hymns that came to mind, and as they did, we gave them voice. No one wanted to be the first to leave. We closed with "Spirit of the living God, fall afresh on me."

The family singing through our tears

That was then. This time Mom asked, remembering that impromptu gathering, "For old times' sake, let's sing 'Spirit of the Living God.'" But I couldn't do it. I couldn't find the first note. Still introspective—no, emotionally paralyzed—I couldn't bear the thought of sound, especially our sounds. We aren't strong singers, though we both love music and gustily join in whenever we're in a singing group large enough that nobody can really hear *us*. Holidays will find us gathered around a piano, booming forth—well, Mom sings; I do the booming forth.

But not today, on this return to the Rock, just the two of us. I couldn't do it. I hated to disappoint yet again, but I couldn't do it. Only silence was seemly; it was all I could give.

It wouldn't last forever, this muteness. I would look forward to coming back to The Rock one day, maybe even soon, when like your mother I could reflect with more gratitude than anguish. There had been much healing already, enough promises of stronger days to come, to give me hope.

And, in time, hope returned.

What I really want now is one more hug. It would be a long one.

Thanks, Son. We needed to talk.

Printed in the USA
CPSIA information can be obtained
at www.ICGtesting.com
CBHW021805280424
7689CB00002B/30

9 781666 761399